HOW (NOT) TO BE A LEADER

From the **HOW-NOT-TO GUIDES FOR LEADERS** Series

HOW (NOT) TO BE A LEADER

MARY E. MARSHALL & KIM OBBINK

Indigo River Publishing

How (NOT) To Be A Leader

© 2020 by Mary E. Marshall and Kim Obbink

All rights reserved. No portion of this publication may be reproduced, stored in a retrieval system, or transmitted by any means—electronic, mechanical, photocopying, recording, or any other—except for brief quotations in printed reviews, without the prior written permission of the publisher.

Edited by Tanner Chau, Joshua Owens, and Regina Cornell
Cover and interior design by Robin Vuchnich
Illustrations by Joe Anderson

Indigo River Publishing
3 West Garden Street, Ste. 718
Pensacola, FL 32502
www.indigoriverpublishing.com

Ordering Information:

Quantity sales: Special discounts are available on quantity purchases by corporations, associations, and others. For details, contact the publisher at the address above.

Orders by US trade bookstores and wholesalers: Please contact the publisher at the address above.

Printed in the United States of America

Library of Congress Control Number: 2019957575

ISBN: 978-1-950906-38-3 (paperback), 978-1-950906-43-7 (ebook)

First Edition

With Indigo River Publishing, you can always expect great books, strong voices, and meaningful messages. Most importantly, you'll always find...words worth reading.

CONTENTS

PREFACE   IX

SECTION 1:
DEBUNKING THE STEREOTYPE

Now You're Bossing!   1
Ch. 1:   Flaunt Your Wealth, You've Earned It!   3
Ch. 2:   One-To-Ones: You + You = 3   7
Ch. 3:   You're The Smartest Person In The Room   11
Ch. 4:   I'm Sorry...What?   15
Ch. 5:   It's All About You   19
Ch. 6:   You Have All The Answers   23
Ch. 7:   Large And In Charge   27
Ch. 8:   Playing With Power   31

SECTION 2:
VALUING YOUR VALUES

There's An Elephant's Asshole In The Room   37
Ch. 9:   The Irrelevance Of Truth   41
Ch. 10: Make Sure Everyone Knows When You're Upset   45
Ch. 11: Show Up As Anyone But Yourself   49
Ch. 12: Drop Your Integrity   53
Ch. 13: Be Loved   57
Ch. 14: Managing Your Personal Brand   61
Ch. 15: Evil Rules   67
Ch. 16: Tears: Your Power Drug   71

SECTION 3: LEADING BY EXAMPLE

The Road To Hell, Perfectly Paved By You	77
Ch. 17: Micromanage The Shit Out Of Everything	81
Ch. 18: Be Best Buds	85
Ch. 19: Follow The Leader	89
Ch. 20: The Waiting Game	93
Ch. 21: Winning The Blame Game	99
Ch. 22: Hazing As An Art Form	103
Ch. 23: Gender Matters	107
Ch. 24: Hub And Spokin'	111

PREVIEW:

"How (NOT) To Build A Great Team"	115

ABOUT THE AUTHORS

117

PREFACE

***How (NOT) To Be A Leader* is the first in a series of how-not-to guides for newly minted leaders** looking to avoid becoming feared or hated losers in the ivory tower or veteran leaders looking in the rearview mirror wondering where and why they ran off the road. Irreverent and hilarious, *How (NOT) To Be A Leader* shines a big bright spotlight on the oh-so-common mistakes that many leaders make when they plow forward through life and business without taking the time to really consider the effect their leadership is having on others. We've all seen and heard the horror stories of bad leadership, and hopefully many of us have been lucky enough to have been the benefactor of truly great leadership. Either way, if it's your turn at the top, *How (NOT) To Be A Leader* will help you understand what you can do to be a better leader by first understanding what you should never ever do; and if you are, why you should back up the truck, take another look at yourself and your leadership qualities, and do the work and self-reflection needed to get back on track.

Why this book series? Having been in the leadership trenches for a combined fifty years, we've seen a lot. Some good, some bad, and some really, really horrible. There was no guide for us, and we want to help all those leaders who will come after us. Not with a boring manifesto about a fictional leader who only exists in a book, but with real-life stories we've experienced or even perpetrated ourselves and vow never to repeat.

This book consists of twenty-four characteristics that you don't want to be known for. Not all twenty-four will apply to you and a few might resonate louder than others. What was it you heard in your last 360? Micromanaging doesn't work? You aren't listening? You want everyone to do it your way? You might have a few to work on, and our challenge to you is to choose three or four that seem the most immediate and start working on those. Once you've mastered them, take on a few more. And certainly share the book with those around you whose leadership styles need a little polish.

Should you accept this leadership challenge, you will be able to quickly identify twenty-four ineffective leadership traits and make changes to positively address them. Through the stories in this book, you will learn how to avoid the pitfalls of leadership, how to be a better leader, and, most importantly, how to pass good leadership on to those you lead.

SECTION 1

DEBUNKING THE STEREOTYPE

INTRODUCTION

NOW YOU'RE BOSSING!

What does good leadership mean? That's a tough question to answer. Usually it depends upon who's speaking, and then it depends upon their own personal experiences. Context matters.

The myth is that leaders need to be tough, driven, hard edged, and even ruthless. If you subscribe to this myth, you might have crushed a few bodies on the way up the ladder with the belief that, no matter the means, the reward of the corner office or title was worth the trip. This attitude says that it's all about the toys you can accumulate with the money you make off the work of others. It tells you that it's okay to have an oversized ego, to take credit for the work of others, and to behave in ways that your mama would not be proud of, all in the name of leadership.

The reality is that there are leaders out there who behave like this. They don't lead successfully for very long, but they do lead, or more accurately, they command. Because of the power position they hold, for whatever dubious reason people will obey. Held hostage by salary, family obligations, or simple lethargy about changing jobs, people put up with all kinds of appalling leadership. Let's be clear: this is not leadership, it's closer to dictatorship. Do as I say not as I do or else.

On the flip side, good leaders inspire, mentor, and truly lead. They are not all about themselves, they are about the mission. They don't flaunt their wealth, they share it with those who took them to the top. They are not about making sure only their opinion is heard but that all ideas are heard and valued. They are about truly listening to what is being said instead of waiting to talk. They are about surrounding themselves with bright and eager talent, especially if those people know more than they do. They are not about being all powerful; they are about empowering others to do well by doing good.

Almost everyone has had some experience with both types of leaders. Chances are you learned most of what you know about leadership from whichever type you had. Or maybe you learned about leadership from those crazy reality TV shows, which have absolutely nothing whatsoever to do with real leadership.

The bottom line is that the leaders who get the best results are not those who behave with ego first and everyone else last. The best leaders are those whose vision and ethics are clear and known to all, whose emotional intelligence is high, and for whom self-reflection is about the effect they are having on others and not how amazing they look to themselves in the mirror. As leaders, we all have a responsibility to debunk the despicable boss stereotype of the past and evolve forward to being leaders who have a positive effect on the lives of those we lead. As Gandhi once said, "There goes my people. I must follow them, for I am their leader."

CHAPTER 1

FLAUNT YOUR WEALTH, YOU'VE EARNED IT!

Sent: Sunday, July 9 at 2:31 am
To: ALL STAFF
From: CEO
Subject: I was robbed! In late tomorrow.

I can't believe that some THUG had the audacity to reach down through my sunroof and steal my things right out of my car! My Tiffany bag was on top of my Armani suit bag and they took everything! I'm unbelievably devastated. Need to file a police report first thing in the morning. Thank God for Lloyds of London.

Do not underestimate the power of perception. It's important that as a leader you portray yourself in a light that others not only look up to but aspire to. Wealth, particularly material wealth, is a symbol of success, so be sure to take every opportunity you can to display your wealth. This will be proof to others that, if they simply work as hard as you do, and are as smart as you are, they too can also (someday maybe) have the things that you have. It's a stretch, but let them dream.

Let's start with how you look and how you dress. All aspects of your appearance should be attended to weekly. This not only indicates that you have the money to do this but that you also have the time. Your subordinates will feel honored that their hard work allows you to take good care of yourself, so be sure to mention your weekly self-care appointments and always make these appointments a priority over all else.

When assembling your office wardrobe, there is one rule of thumb: brands, big brands. Dressing in brands that are normally reserved for Hollywood's rich and famous will quickly set you worlds apart from your staff. This is just the start in making your personal lifestyle both aspirational and mysterious. A general rule of thumb is to wear $3,000 to $5,000 top to bottom every day (not including accessories). This means high-end name brands only, not department store garbage. And of course, for that special meeting with the venture-capital crew of the opposite sex, nothing says power like classic black with a big red statement. Diamonds on your ears or cuffs, not on your finger please, because when you need money, you need to look available!

Now, on to your residential status. You absolutely must live in the most affluent zip code in your city. Your home should be very large. These points are nonnegotiable for a leader for many reasons, the first and most important of which is that you need a suitable place to hold all company parties. Holding company events at your home is a sure-fire way to keep the appropriate distance from your staff. Again, your job is to be a role model of material success. Only you can create this persona, so do it well and do your best to overdo it! Really, if you go big here, you can't go wrong.

If you have children, make sure that it appears as if they are well cared for by someone other than you. This will ensure that others see you as someone who is simply too important and busy for day-to-day matters. In fact, doing this makes you look like a master of outsourcing. But of course, have the requisite children to make it look like you actually care about something other than yourself. Make sure your home staff is present and scurrying about during any company event and that they address you as Ms./Mr., not by your first name (if only your company staff would do this!). Also make sure that your company events are catered by only the best, that there are fresh flowers in every room, and that (for that extra zinger) you have hired a valet to park your company staffs' Hyundais far, far away. Remember: your primary home is a showpiece for your staff and your business colleagues, your vacation homes are for you.

Lastly, let's discuss your car. Eighty thousand is the minimum you should expend on this extremely important investment. And make no mistake, it's an investment. Nothing screams success like a top-of-the-line Mercedes (no more than two years old and leased so you can upgrade regularly). It's not just a three-pointed-star logo, it's a symbol of innovation, performance, and design. Just. Like. You. And don't forget to have an assigned parking space with your name or title on it. Your investment needs a spot of its own, and you need to show everyone how it's done!

Wear it, live in it, drive it, baby! If you follow these simple guidelines, you'll not only be a great leader, you'll look and act like one too.

LET'S GET REAL

Please. Be humble. Flaunting your wealth will alienate you from your staff. Make no mistake, they may ooh and ahh at your fancy digs, but they will secretly and absolutely hate you and see you as nothing more than a haughty snob. The greatest leaders of all time have been those who care passionately and genuinely about the well-being of the people they employ. If you only care about your personal gain, please go do something else that doesn't include employing people. You're making it too hard for those who actually care.

Leadership is not about what you have, it's about what you do. The more emphasis you place on things, the less your employees will care about you and what your company is trying to do. They want to work for a company whose mission is bigger than making you rich. If it's all about making you rich, they will either decide to leave or they will make sure you don't stay rich.

CHAPTER 2

ONE-TO-ONES: YOU + YOU = 3

**NOTE TO SELF:
SET RECURRING ONE-TO-ONE MEETINGS WITH MYSELF.**

So much happens in the daily life of a leader that it's important that you carve out time for yourself. As we've discussed, the best answers come from you, so why not spend some time working on that. And when we use the word work, it's not really work, because, let's face it, those good ideas just come to you because you have an above-average if not brilliant brain, right?

It's important that you make it a weekly recurring meeting, preferably on a Friday afternoon, say, after lunch. Schedule at least three hours because you don't know how long the process will take each week.

You can have this meeting with yourself anywhere: over a mani-pedi or a good massage, on the golf course, at a bar, in your car, literally anywhere you happen to be. The purpose of booking the room at your club is so that it *looks* like you've thought this out and take it seriously. The important part is that you get alone with your thoughts and really assess how you're doing as a leader. Ask yourself the following questions:

- How would you rate yourself on your leadership skills overall (remember, giving yourself a negative rating or being humble is for losers)?

    Good
    Above average
    Excellent

- What good examples of leadership do you have from this week (that you can claim credit for)?

- Who had a good idea that you can use?

- Who questioned your leadership?

- What persistent problems should you blame on one of your team?

- Who might need to be taken down a peg?

- What can you brag about this week (leading by example)?

You'll be surprised by how quickly the answers come to you, and you'll have a whole set of action items to move forward on. But don't get carried away. Don't bother writing all your ideas down, especially if you're doing the mani-pedi one-to-one (your hands will be occupied!). You'll remember the best ones and know what to implement next week because it's what comes naturally to you.

Most importantly, don't be too hard on yourself. Self-reflection is about basking in the good, not criticizing yourself for perceived errors. Having a one-to-one with yourself is about reinforcing why you are the leader and how you got there. Relive your glory days in your mind and remember that you're still that person. Boost your confidence by reveling in all you own, all you've done, and how much your people love you. You're their leader and they know it!

This is a time to recharge your leadership chops by thinking about yourself. This will, by extension, help your team, but first and foremost it's for you. If there were someone else in the company who had better ideas than yours, that would be a threat, so there's no point in bringing anyone else into this brainstorming session. Your one-to-one with yourself also shows your team that you take your job seriously: that you give considerable thought and attention to the leadership challenges of the day.

Occasionally you can use this time to read up on the latest trends in leadership or your industry, but don't make this a habit. Remember, you know what to do by either looking backward or at what you feel in the moment so there's no point in paying too much attention to forward trends. Let someone else be first to work out the kinks. Nonetheless, you will want to take a business book or magazine with you so it looks like you pay attention to this stuff. Make a point of showing it to your executive team. One of the butt kissers will read it and tell you all about it, so what's the point of reading it first?

So get away, refresh, and remind yourself weekly why you're a good leader!

LET'S GET REAL

A one-to-one with yourself happens every minute of every day. Carving out fake time for it just reinforces that you do not value others' opinions and that yours is the most important in the room. One-to-ones with your team members are valuable, both for getting help and insight and for giving them. If you always have all the ideas, your team will be fearful of offering opinions, and eventually they will stop. Teams that don't discuss new ideas, or that only discuss those of their leader, eventually fail.

Getting insights from as many people as possible and distilling the information down to what's useful is a sign of a good leader. Coaches, mentors, and board members can all be very helpful in your leadership role. Having your own assumptions challenged by others will lead to better outcomes. Your team can be encouraged to challenge your ideas, and the result is learning for the entire team and, almost always, better ideas. The right insights are not always yours.

CHAPTER 3

YOU'RE THE SMARTEST PERSON IN THE ROOM

Sent: Monday, July 25 at 8:30 am
From: CEO
To: Executive Team
Subject: My Ideas

Meet me in the conference room at 9:00 am as I have some great ideas of mine that I want to share with you.

One of the benefits of being a great leader is always being the smartest person in the room. It's important to maintain that brilliance and, more importantly, to make sure everyone else sees it. After all, if the rest of them were as smart as you, they'd be in charge, wouldn't they? Look at where they are and where you are. Pretty easy equation.

So let's talk about how you stay on top of this amazing gift you have to impart: your perceived intelligence. First, flaunt it at every step. For example, if there is a meeting or conversation going on and you know even a little bit about the topic, jump in with a random factoid (it doesn't need to be a factual factoid, however) that shows you're the expert. When you spout factoids of your own making (loudly and with confidence and authority) no one will dare question you. And if you do it repeatedly, you'll build the muscle memory that helps them remember that everything you say is true.

If someone dares contradict you, stand your ground, for this is brilliance in and of itself. Defend, defend, defend. A leader never gives any ground as doing so would cause those you lead to question you, which is completely unacceptable.

Occasionally, you will find that some in the room have more education than you or others, in rare cases, might even be right. The way to deal with them is twofold: First, ask yourself why you hired them in the first place, and never make that mistake again. Second, reassert your dominance through volume and interruption immediately. Let them continue talking, but interrupt by randomly peppering them with questions so that they become flustered. Then tell them to get their facts straight next time and leave it at that.

Another approach for dealing with this type of annoyance is to be very quiet while they talk. Let them finish, then slowly start clapping your hands. When you have everyone's attention, say to this person: "You get the gold star today. I was purposely waiting for one of you to come up with the right solution and you did it! I knew the answer, but I wanted to see if any of you were fast enough to pick up on my clues." This will blow them away every time, and you get to claim their idea while maintaining your status as the most brilliant person in the room. Mirror, mirror on the wall, why do they even try?

The final point on maintaining your brilliance is that you need to be very careful when hiring. You do not need anyone smarter than you around, so if a candidate seems even remotely better educated, more knowledgeable, more experienced, or in any way smarter than you, don't hire them. Never ever hire anyone who might be perceived as smarter than you. Why risk it?

LET'S GET REAL

Great leaders recognize their own strengths and weaknesses and surround themselves with talented team members who complement those strengths and weaknesses and those of other colleagues. Growth and innovation is born out of everyone learning from one another in a never-ending cycle of mentorship. If you are arrogant enough to believe that you have all the answers or are always right, you will stunt or prevent both the personal enrichment of your people and the positive evolution of your organization.

Your job as a leader is to focus and shine light on the contributions of others, not yourself. If you need validation and seek it from within your organization, you may not be ready for true leadership. Genuine leaders are validated by facilitating others' success. If you need a pat on the back, reach right around and give it to yourself. Good job!

CHAPTER 4

I'M SORRY...WHAT?

Sent: Monday, September 6 at 11:14 pm
From: CEO
To: Bev
Subject: What's up?

Bev, you wanted to tell me something? Just leave me a note with whatever it was. I'll let you know if it needs a response.

Thx.

As the leader, you need to *pretend* to listen to your people, but really you're using your time much more productively. There is a lot of talk these days about leaders being good listeners. But really that's just BS because leaders are good tellers. Your people are looking to you to tell them what to do. Besides, what could they possibly have to say that you would be interested in hearing?

The current buzz word is *active listening*. In fact *inactive listening* is actually more productive and more suited to a good leader. (Note to self: get a trademark on that phrase. Brilliant!) What this means is that you appear to be listening but you're not. First, it's important to look at the other person for a least a couple of seconds of the exchange, but God forbid, don't try to make eye contact because that's just awkward and weird. Once you've made that initial head shake of listening, just drown out that annoying voice with thoughts about what else you have going on.

This is a great time for you to look around your office and think about what needs redoing or redecorating (it's always important to have a sharp-looking office), make your shopping list, or consider the things you really need to do (like make that appointment to get a haircut). When you've had enough of the patter and your lists are made, break out of your thoughts and say, "Give me the bullets, please." This way the other person will have to summarize and you'll get the gist of whatever they were blabbing on about.

If, for some reason, you can't seem to grasp what they are saying or you just plain don't care, ask them to summarize it in an email and send it to you so you can "think on it." This always works well, and they are so pleased that you not only listened but think it's worthy of a follow up email. And don't worry, there's no need to actually read or follow up on that email. Remember, you're a very busy leader.

Another great strategy for inactive listening is to let the person go on and on, and when you're bored, say, "I'm sorry, what?" This lets them know you were paying attention but want them to repeat a point. It definitely shows them you care, and empathy is always a sign of a good leader! And the best part is, it's only three words, saving you from actually having to have a conversation.

Always remember that when someone comes to talk to you, they really came to listen to you. They want to hear what you have to say on whatever subject they're talking about. You're the expert—why wouldn't they want to listen? So, after you've let them go on for a few minutes, cut them off and offer your words of wisdom on the subject, even if you don't know what the hell they were talking about. They just took up your time, now they can listen. And if they're loyal, they'll pick up a few tips they can use.

When sharing your wisdom, be sure to give as much or as little detail as you want. Sometimes it's just nice to hear your own voice. You might even sound more brilliant than you already thought you were, and that's always a pleasant sound. If you don't know the subject well, make stuff up because most people are sheep and they don't want to know the truth, they just want to know what you have to say and hear how you say it. Use big, generic words that are nonspecific and that can be applied to anything and anyone: words like *fantastic*, *great*, *amazing*, *terrific*, and *huge*.

There are a couple of pitfalls you want to avoid in inactive listening. First, never get too interested in the topic unless it's gossip about someone that you can use for your own purposes down the road. If it's gossip, press the talker for all the dirt they have because, as the leader, it's important that you know this and it's important that they know they can come dish to you anytime, like whenever they get a juicy tidbit.

The second pitfall is actually listening. You can get caught up in what the other person is telling you and actually forget that you don't care, which then makes them think you care. This is the death knell for a leader. It means you let your guard down, and they might think you are actually learning from or interested in something they have to say, which makes you weak. So, if you find yourself actually interested in something they are saying, look at your watch and let them know you have to go so they have a minute to wrap up. Tell them to send you a summary of whatever they were talking about, and if it's good, use it at the next management meeting as your idea. Gets 'em every time!

LET'S GET REAL

As a leader, your job is to listen. People will not follow you or respect you if you don't care, and listening is a tangible way of caring about the speaker. Your job as a good leader is to mentor and teach all the time, and if you don't listen, you cannot possibly know how to mentor someone. This is empathy in action, but empathy doesn't necessarily mean that you have to take action on someone's behalf.

Your instinct will be to solve whatever the problem is, but that's not listening. Listen, ask questions, and help the other person solve the problem by talking it through. You can only do this through active listening, and there is no faking it. Active listening means not waiting to talk and not playing the tape in your head of a similar incident that you can share. It means being fully present to what's being said. It means having empathy and also listening to what's not being said. Ask questions, really trying to understand where the speaker is coming from and understand what they want or need from you. As a leader, it's also your job to learn, and the more you listen, the more you learn.

CHAPTER 5

IT'S ALL ABOUT YOU

Sent: Tuesday, December 31 at 4:00 pm
From: CEO/President
To: Gary B., VP Sales & Marketing
Subject: My feedback

I understand that you wanted me to wait for you on this, but that didn't seem like a good idea to me. So while you were on vacation I went ahead and had the agency present me with their concepts for the spring campaign you asked them to work on. I'm leaving you this feedback since I'll be on my semi-annual cruise when you get back—this way you can make revisions for me to look at once I've recovered from what I'm sure is going to be a nonstop party!

Frankly, I hate the creative. I get that it's strategic and the messaging targets our new demographic, but I just don't think the ideas are good ideas. The headlines sound like something my ex-wife would say and I just can't get that out of my head. Also, I've never liked yellow (studies show that most men don't so I'm not sure why you chose it) so the color scheme has to change.

Also, I haven't had the time to tell you this, but I'm up for a Marketing Innovation Award this year. I thought it would be more impactful to have the CEO on the nomination instead of VP of Marketing. I'm sure you'd agree. That said, it's important that they get this creative where I want it. I can't be embarrassed by shoddy creative at this prestigious award ceremony. The one category missing from my awards list is marketing, so I'm planning on winning this year.

Make it happen for me buddy!

Now this is putting your best leadership foot forward! It takes courage to tell it like it is. Ask for what you want. Better yet, demand what you want and expect nothing less. Remind yourself daily that this organization would not be what it is today without you—your intuition, your gut, your determination, and your selfless commitment to excellence. Your people need to know that the organization is a direct reflection of your exacting standards and yours alone. So make sure everyone knows where your bar is, then revel in watching them try to reach it.

As the ultimate leader, it's also important to make sure that your team understands that your calendar comes first, and you need think time first and foremost. Once you've established this, it won't be a surprise to them if you are unavailable when they need you or if they are forced to reengineer schedules for their own teams, vendors, or others. These are the problems you pay them to solve, so let them solve them. You simply don't have time to do their thinking for them.

Recognition—your recognition—is an important way both to secure the hierarchy you've worked so hard to achieve and to keep your competitors and other industry leaders believing that you are running the show (see Chapter 14: Managing Your Personal Brand), so be careful to give credit where credit is due: to you. You've paid your dues to get where you are, now reap the rewards!

Remember, it's all about you. If it wasn't for you, there would be no them.

LET'S GET REAL

Narcissistic Personality Disorder: People with narcissistic personalities really believe that the world revolves around them. They lack all ability to empathize and they have a deep and desperate need to keep the attention and focus on themselves.

This disorder is expressed through arrogant and self-serving behavior, and a lack of empathy for others. Narcissists need to be admired, revered, and respected at all times and often display overly confident, egomaniacal, and manipulative behavior. People with this disorder often times have lofty unattainable goals of fame or fortune, and they demand that those around them also work toward those goals.

Congratulations! If the email at the beginning of this chapter sounds like you, we've just saved you a ton of money in therapy fees trying to figure out why nobody really respects or likes you. And, if you don't recognize and change your behavior, that won't be the only expense you're likely to incur. Narcissistic behavior in leadership is one of the most common causes of dissent amongst employees. Where it's present, more often than not an employee may love the company, love their job, but ultimately their disrespect and dislike for you causes them to run for the hills.

Empathy is the key word here, and lack of empathy is at the center of narcissism and narcissistic behavior. Great leaders are empathetic in that they have the capacity to understand, share, and prioritize others' feelings and emotions. Your level of empathy is directly related to your ability to understand not only the needs of your employees but the needs of your customers. In the case of your organization and those you lead, you will not be able to build a cohesive team or gain trust if you lack empathy. In the case of your customers, without empathy you will not be able to create business strategies for products or services that satisfy them.

So maybe it is all about you. Because if you're a narcissist, it's your lack of empathy that will lead to the failure of others and your business.

CHAPTER 6

YOU HAVE ALL THE ANSWERS

Sent: Wednesday, July 4 at 10:08 pm
From: CEO
To: Executive Team
Subject: Mind Map Session

A reminder to everyone that tomorrow is our mind map session for our new product line. Please be prepared to discuss all your ideas related to the subject. Don't bring any notes because I want to see how much you can retain and think outside the box.

After the session I'll expect a full report from each of you so we can compare the takeaways.

As the leader it's your job to have the answers, because you don't pay your people to think, you pay them to do. You will waste valuable time and money struggling to execute other people's flawed ideas, so keep your people focused on your vision, and tell them exactly how to do what needs to be done to get there.

How do you get all those answers? Well, it's tricky, but you get them from your team without them knowing about it. One sure-fire method for extracting ideas and answers from an unsuspecting team is to facilitate a mind-map session. You can learn more about this technique by Googling it and spending thirty or forty seconds reading about it, but essentially it's a method to solve problems without participating in the solution yourself. Bring everyone together and put the problem on the table. Go around the table making each person write the next thing they think about as it relates to the problem.

Keep doing this with each person pinging off the one before them—somewhere in there someone will come up with a good idea. Your job is to pluck out that good idea and start the process again by mind mapping off that. You do not need consensus or agreement as to whether or not the idea is a good one; instead, take immediate credit for it by saying something like, "That's exactly what I was thinking. I'm glad you agree." Or, "I was hoping someone would bring that up; it's so obvious to me." Then rinse and repeat.

Everyone but you should have been taking copious notes as you instructed them to, so once the mind-map session is complete, you can select the best notes with the most detail and assign the implementation of the solution to that person. You now have the ability to take credit for the process, the ideas, and the masterful delegation of the work that lies ahead. This is leadership at its best.

If you're concerned that the person you delegated your ideas to doesn't feel validated or feels like you're taking credit for their work, simply follow up with some positive, leaderly reinforcement statements. You can say things like:

- You know you're my favorite right?
- Did you see how I was leading you to that answer?

- I love how you enhanced my original idea.

- It's great that you learned from my brainstorming techniques.

- I'm impressed that you noticed that I gave you the answer in my questions.

Remember: have all the answers and keep the pecking order in check, and you will always be seen as the smartest person in the room.

LET'S GET REAL

As the leader you don't have all the answers, and righteousness only makes you wrong even when you're right. Your job is to empower others and be the facilitator or mentor for a better solution by leading the team to their own solutions, not corralling them to yours. When someone comes to you with a problem, first ask them what solutions they have thought through. Tell them you are happy to talk it out with them, but you want them to come up with an answer or two and you'll help work out the best solution. When you mentor your people to the right answer rather than solving the problem yourself, they'll feel more empowered and confident to find solutions in the future.

Great leaders encourage the contribution of ideas and solutions from their teams and commit to helping see them through to ensure their success. Don't try to prove them wrong or hunt for opportunities to say, "I told you so." Occasionally you will need to support ideas that you might not entirely agree with, but if and when those ideas fail, you will fail together. You would want the same if you asked your people to follow through with something you felt strongly about that failed or had a different-than-expected outcome. Remember: the only thing that's worse than failure, is failing alone. And that is the result of righteousness.

CHAPTER 7

LARGE AND IN CHARGE

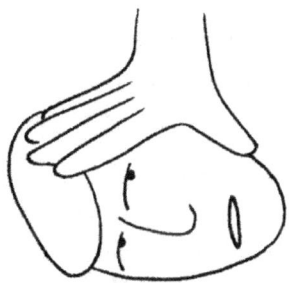

Sent: Monday, March 16 at 5:47 pm
From: CEO's Desk
To: Executive Team
Subject: Investment Banker Presentation on Tues.

Team,

The folks from Gold Tower Investments will be here on Tuesday as part of their vetting process is to meet with all of you, get to know you better individually, and get a real sense of the strength and valuable contribution that each of you bring to our great company. Please be early and bring your best! Also, seating and presentation is important in this meeting, so I'll be seated at the head of the conference table. Jim, Dave, and Bill, I'd like you on my left representing business and finance. Ladies, if you would please sit together on my right representing HR and marketing. All of you, dress for success. Ladies, NO pantsuits!

I'll assume that we all agree I'll answer ALL the questions, unless I specifically ask you something or turn in your direction. You need to be prepared for any and all questions when and if I call on you to answer on your own behalf. Please stay bright-eyed and attentive as they're expecting you to be the A team!

See you all then, and best of luck to you!

Body language and physical presentation are critical to great leadership, not only when presenting to others but also in your day-to-day encounters with your staff to ensure that you are at all times positioned in a way that reinforces your authority. Let's start with body language. There are two easy words to keep top of mind: height and proximity. Studies in business books have shown that tall people emanate power and are especially fortunate to have that natural intimidation factor working in their favor. For those less fortunate (which is anyone under 5' 9" in the United States) you will have to find ways to appear taller. For women, this means the highest heels that you can stay balanced in. Since anything under a 3" heel tends to look dowdy and age you, shoot for 3.5" and higher. Four inches is the optimal heel height to both increase your height and say, "I'm in charge and can get nasty when I need to" at the same. For men who fall short (pun intended!) of optimum power height, there's an old adage: "When you can't go high, go wide!" So hit the gym, bulk up, and make sure that your upper arms and shoulders are as wide and muscular as possible. This will say to everyone in the room, "I may be short, but I'll kick your ass to get my way, and I'm so awesome that I have lots of free time to spend in the gym." Also shoe lifts can work, but make sure it isn't obvious that you're wearing them. And for God's sake, if you have small hands, keep them under the table. No sense in advertising that! Women, if you have a decent rack, let it show! It will keep the focus on your boobs and you're more likely to get what you want. You might as well use all your assets!

Once you have reached the optimum stature, you'll want

to work on your proximity to others. Remember that a surefire way to state your position is to invade your subordinates' personal space. After all, they are your employees: you gave them the space they are occupying, so it's yours to claim as you see fit. When visiting a team member's office, stand or loom over them. If you need to sit, perch on their desk near their chair so as to say, "Look only at me, and listen only to me." Planting yourself directly on top of their working files is also a way to subliminally let them know what you think of their most recent SWOT analysis or competitive review. This will have them shaking in their boots about that upcoming performance review! Your invasion of their personal space with all parts of your body can be oppressive, which is the point. Make your people feel your presence—make them feel small and scared.

In a group setting, this dynamic is even more critical. But since you are the leader and it's important that you arrive late to most group meetings (see Chapter 20: The Waiting Game), you may have to get creative to ensure that you have the most visible seat at the head of the table. Techniques for doing this include simply approaching the person sitting in your desired seat, looming over them, and saying nothing. This creates a healthy, natural tension that will cause them to offer you their seat at once. You can also announce that you'd like to rearrange the seating and move everyone to the seat you would like them to sit in. When meeting with investors, bankers, strategic partners, etc., make absolutely certain that you seat the most attractive team members nearest your guests (second to you, of course), but whatever you do, don't let them speak.

Over time, you will learn the other subtleties of body language for leadership: waving your arms, slamming your palm on your desk, rolling your eyes, giving squinty stares, and making long, breathy sighs. Every body movement, or lack thereof, is powerful! These are all techniques to get your point across without wasting your words. Remember: intimidating silence is golden!

LET'S GET REAL

Leaders are often the last to fully realize how their body language and interpersonal behavior is interpreted by others and how it can create an unspoken barrier between them and their colleagues. Frequently your body language is the first thing to make you appear inaccessible, dominating, or intimidating. So remember: make meaningful eye contact when you're listening, never stand over anyone, respect others' personal space, and let people speak for themselves.

Great leadership means putting others before your self and giving them the space they need to grow. Being aware of your own physical presence, your hand gestures, and your proximity to others is respectful and necessary. All of these unspoken cues will cause others to feel either intimidated or welcomed and encouraged. Be mindful of your space and how much oxygen you are giving or taking in any given setting. Others are watching closely.

CHAPTER 8

PLAYING WITH POWER

Sent: Sunday, April 8 at 11:40 pm
From: CEO
To: Exec Team
Subject: Meeting

Please come to tomorrow's meeting prepared to discuss one thing you would like one of your colleagues to change. There has been lot of backbiting lately as several of you have reported to me, so it's time to get it out in the open. Should be an interesting discussion.

One of the best things about being a leader is the power that what you say goes. You have the ability to easily make or break someone and to have a little fun in the process. Power is the ultimate weapon! The challenge is having it come off as sincere and realistic, as if you had to do it.

An example of this would be to have your direct reports tell you what their career goals are. Encourage them to be as honest as they possibly can, even going so far as to offer up your job to them as an enticement to talk. For example, you could say something like, "What if I were to leave or be promoted, would you want this role?" This a great way to suss out those who might be disloyal to you. You'll want to listen to their answers carefully. Do they praise you and say there is no way they could ever do your job? That's a keeper. If they do see themselves in your role, keep that to yourself for future use. You can cut them down in public with that little tidbit when it will hurt most. Finding others' vulnerabilities is the key to great leadership.

Here's where you need to be strategic about things. You will often have to wait several weeks or even months for just the right time to embarrass, mock, or humiliate someone who deserves it. Patience is great virtue when using power to your advantage. However, if the perfect opportunity doesn't present itself before you run the risk of forgetting what you were going to use, call a meeting! Set everyone up for a catfight and let the fur fly. Even if the premise of the meeting has nothing to do with what you want to embarrass someone with, it's your meeting and you can rain on the parade. And rain you will. The poor unsuspecting sops will never know what hit them.

Let's say you called the meeting to discuss conversations that had been going on recently. Even if there had been none, you can bet that someone will bring something up. Let them go on for awhile attacking each other. Wait until someone else attacks your prey and then pounce. Throw out what you know about them, what they told you in confidence, or something else you know would be humiliating, embarrassing, or just plain mean. Whether it's true or not doesn't matter. You're the leader and what you say and how you say is all the truth you need.

As a leader, you also need to make public displays of power. The reasons are irrelevant, but these displays become your chance to publically humiliate people, and that's the power move. Later, if anyone has the audacity to challenge you, you can privately lay them out and they become your next public victim. Pretty soon, no one will ever question you, which is exactly what you want. A culture of fear, intimidation, and unpredictability is the most productive of all. Most importantly, this type of culture ensures that you are the only one who truly and skillfully can wield the power. Only you have the sword. You will be on fire, so much so that you'll need a cigarette after your performance (which was almost better than sex after all)!

On occasion, you might have a few sad sacks who feel the need to come to the rescue of the one you're abusing. Again, if they do it publically, take them down swiftly and succinctly just like you did the first one. Never tolerate any vulnerability or empathy in your team. Those are traits of losers, not leaders.

This is how you use power: to get what you want, to crush those who threaten you, and to just generally play with people because you can. It really feels good. The best part is everybody wants to be you—they want to be the one wielding the invisible power wand. You can never have enough because power begets power and the more you use it, the more you'll get. So c'mon, get on the power train. You'll never get off!

LET'S GET REAL

Never use power to humiliate, embarrass, or otherwise demean another human being either privately or publicly. Doing so just makes you look small, pathetic, and weak. Power is a tool to be used for doing what's right for the individual, the whole, and the greater good. Unfortunately, when some leaders get power, it goes to their heads and the only thing they can focus on is keeping it, hence the roadkill along the way. Exploiting someone's vulnerability is not leadership, it's abuse. Name-calling or belittling someone says more about the perpetrator than it does about the victim. What you call someone is usually what you are or what you fear. Words matter.

Being a power-hungry leader will get you the reputation of being an asshole and lead to dismal results. Real results come from using your power wisely: making good decisions, promoting those who do good work, acknowledging that work, helping others achieve their career goals, and never being afraid to do so. A good leader almost never uses power but rather leads and guides the organization to success through the successes of others and those of the team. Remember the phrase: "Power corrupts; absolute power corrupts absolutely." Very true.

SECTION TWO

VALUING YOUR VALUES

INTRODUCTION
THERE'S AN ELEPHANT'S ASSHOLE IN THE ROOM

Oh, how many times have we heard this one: "Our culture is dysfunctional and our business is suffering. Let's come up with some core values and make people live by them. That'll fix everything."

We've all seen it, heard it, and read about it: companies whose management has randomly come up with a set of meaningless adjectives, slapped them on some posters in the office, and then never talked about them again. Suddenly the office is plastered with silly motivational posters to remind everyone of guidelines for what amounts to the most basic commonsense principles of business: teamwork, collaboration, innovation, profitability. Yay, and duh. Sometimes these are lofty exclamations better suited for T-shirts such as "Be Awesome!" or "Save the Planet!" Or, worse yet, they're goals and directives not so cleverly masked as core company values such as "Be a Winner!" or "Crush the Competition." These are not values, these are merely words, and they are as vacuous as the souls of the leaders who think they are values. Values matter, posters and words without meaning don't.

The only thing worse than having meaningless or empty values is having no stated values at all, leaving others to wonder what they might be. Not knowing what their leader's ethical platform is (or is not) is terrifying and leaves your people guessing. In an environment of unpredictability, unpredictable things happen. This is not a good business strategy, nor is it leadership. It's a reality TV mentality and has no place in business let alone true leadership.

The healthiest cultures are those where people have an agreed upon set of beliefs that they use as a compass to guide how they act, interact, and make decisions. In functional and intentional cultures, these beliefs are woven into everything the organization does. They are promises to the staff, to the customers, and to the industry, and they should be taken very seriously. They are called core values because they are the most important element of a business strategy: they are the pillars of accountability for each and every member of the organization, and they set the tone for each and every conversation. They are, in a nutshell, the very spirit of the organization: a map or playbook by which its people can successfully operate.

Developing core values should be an inclusive and transparent process that involves as many people as possible. And if done well, it should be a very personal and rewarding journey. How values are developed is every bit as important as how they are expressed and operationalized because consensus and agreement are every bit as important as the values themselves. There are many processes and theories for developing values, but the point we want to make in the following chapters is about you and your role as a leader in developing and maintaining organizational values.

The best leaders are those who have a strong set of personal values and a belief system that they use as a compass to guide their actions, interactions, and decisions. Sound familiar? While a company's stated values should not be a direct reflection of your own personal values (because they should be more inclusive of others), your values and what you stand for should be well known by all. And in order for that to happen, they first must be known by you.

As leaders, we're constantly asking ourselves how our words and actions might be perceived by others. But how often do we put our concerns for simply being perceived as who we really are ahead of our concerns about perceptions? Knowing yourself, getting in touch with your beliefs and your values, and then just simply being that person is not only the easiest thing to do but the noblest. But, once you have done this self-work, once you understand your own compass, then and only then will you be able to be a worthy steward of your company's values. When you're the leader, you get to go first and the company's values, stated or unstated, are a direct reflection of your leadership.

CHAPTER 9

THE IRRELEVANCE OF TRUTH

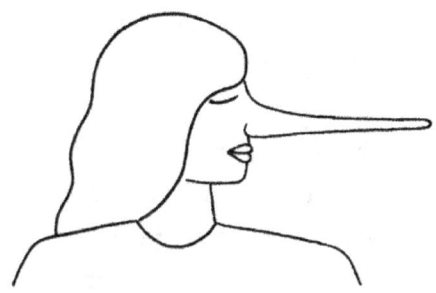

Sent: Tuesday, February 3 at 6:45 pm
From: CEO
To: All Staff
Subject: Difficult Times Ahead

All,

I regret to announce that due to recent decisions by your management team, we're going to be shutting down the San Diego plant. Although this will result in layoffs, all of these people will be offered jobs at our new facility in Fargo, North Dakota. We look forward to our continued growth and profits. The new location offers so much in the way of quality of life and lower cost of living that I'm sure many of you will want to trade your overpriced houses for that much desired white Christmas!

The truth: What is it really? And according to whom? And by the way, exaggeration is not lying, it's just a little aberration on the truth, but it's perfectly acceptable. Remember, there is no actual truth squad, much to some of the elites' dismay.

The point is, you don't need to worry about the truth when you're in pursuit of something. If it gets you what you want, it's the right thing to do: it's your truth that matters. And, because you're the leader, who the hell are they to question you anyway? As we said, the truth is only the truth insofar as it gets you what you want.

When someone is called a liar, it's usually not meant in a positive light. As if they've done something wrong. But seriously, there are about one hundred definitions for lies: little lies, white lies, black lies, lies by omission, lies to spare someone's feelings, whoppers, monsters, prevarications, forgeries, identity theft, untruths, lies of commission, fabrications, errors, restructuring, denial, minimization, and exaggeration, just to name a few. With all of these definitions, how can this be something that is wrong? Clearly, it's a leadership tactic that you must employ.

As a leader, you have to use all the resources at your disposal. Lying is a really good one, and more importantly, it's effective. And it's effective mainly because no one expects leaders to do it, and with the element of surprise, you are successful with it more often than not. If someone does dare to question or confront you, the key is to do one of two things. The first is to own it quickly, explain why it was the right thing to do, then apologize and move on (meaning don't give it another thought). The important thing here is to show why it was the right thing to do: it was a means to an end that was justified. The second is to absolutely deny that you lied and make them think they misunderstood, or, if that doesn't work, just blame someone else. Never admit guilt—that is just a losing strategy.

Remember that all great leaders lie. How else would they have gotten where they are? Take the email at the head of this chapter for example. No one living in San Diego wants to move to North Dakota, even if they do want a white Christmas. But when someone in authority tells you this is the truth, you give it a second look. Then you look for further proof that this might in fact be true. (And let's be clear, you can find any and all points of view on the Internet because conspiracy theories and fake news rule the day.) Before long, you're actually believing that you want to move to North Dakota for a white Christmas, and, oh by the way, for half the pay. See how well that worked?

As a leader, the key is not to give too much information at once. Don't get yourself tripped up right out of the chute. Leave enough wiggle room that you can just make stuff up as needed. Truth is your friend, but stick to it only as long as it serves your purpose.

LET'S GET REAL

The truth is an absolute imperative to great leadership. There are no exceptions to this rule. This does not mean complete and total transparency at all times because you need to be sensitive to privacy and timing and use strategy and tactics to communicate effectively to get the most positive result and reaction. But when you do speak, you must speak the absolute truth and every word that leaves your mouth or your keyboard must be impeccable.

Most human beings default to a trust state when it comes to the internal assessment of leadership. Until that trust is broken. From the very first time that trust is broken, regardless of how minor the break in trust, the default state of those being lead will be fear, mistrust, suspicion, and doubt. As a defense mechanism, those you lead will hunt for and expect lies and untruths, changing the dynamic in a way that can never be repaired. Truthfulness and trustworthiness are the most valuable characteristics of a great leader and should be protected and revered at every step. If not, your lack of these qualities will precede you in every step you take. The result: an abandonment and forfeiture of leadership forever.

CHAPTER 10

MAKE SURE EVERYONE KNOWS WHEN YOU'RE UPSET

Sent: Saturday, August 1 at 6:46 am
From: Management
To: All Staff
Subject: Turnover Rate & Attrition

All,

Yesterday I received our Q2 Turnover & Attrition report and I was ABSOLUTELY HORRIFIED by the data. In the second quarter, we lost 35% of our staff to voluntary resignation and yet another 12% to involuntary termination. This is COMPLETELY UNACCEPTABLE and I hold each and every one of you accountable for these disastrous results. This makes us look like COMPLETE BUFFOONS and our competition is sitting at our front door like HUNGRY WOLVES just waiting for our best talent to walk out where they will be greeted with open arms. I'm sending this to everyone because this is not only the fault of our managers, it's the fault of EACH AND EVERY ONE OF YOU for not creating a better culture and more stable work environment. And I speak on behalf of our entire management team when I say that we EXPECT MORE from all of you. I want these numbers down 50% in Q3!!!! This is not open for discussion and I do not want to hear any excuses.

Enough already goddammit!

As all great leaders know, your temperament is the barometer the entire organization will adjust itself to. And so, it's very important that when you are disappointed, upset, or just plain steaming mad, everyone knows. This can be achieved by your tone, your body language, and your spoken and written language. It is especially effective to communicate your dissatisfaction in emails, texts, and instant messages. Capital letters, underlines, italics, as well as smart and forceful use of punctuation are all useful techniques to put your unwavering passion on display. But nothing puts the cherry on the cake of the moment like a strategically placed expletive. Statements like "This is total bullshit!" or "She can go fuck herself!" or "You're a bunch of goddamn idiots!" are statements that, while shocking in the moment, are totally unforgettable and wildly effective.

When you've had enough of the apathy, excuses, blaming, and sheer laziness that leads to poor business performance, you have no time to waste in making sure everyone knows that you've reached your wit's end. Remember, there is nothing wrong with instilling a little fear into your organization. Fear keeps people on their toes and, more importantly, causes them to do whatever they can to avoid the next verbal smackdown. If, in their minds, that firestorm looms around every corner, then you've got people exactly where you need them.

If you are a business owner, it's especially important that everyone knows the sacrifices you personally have made to create the company. That it's your vision and yours alone, and nothing will stand in the way of its success, especially an apathetic, lazy employee. Putting (and keeping) on your best "How dare you?" attitude will solidify your leadership position, keep them operating at peak performance, and end-run any flare-ups that might be brewing amongst the ranks.

But if you are a member of an executive-management team, there are other techniques you can use to achieve the same effect! You also have the luxury of blaming up and directing your anger at the owner, the investors, or any other person or entity that the staff might believe has authority over you. This preserves the illusion of your loyalty to the staff, so that their love and adoration for you goes unscathed (See Chapter 13: Be Loved) and also gives you one glorious last resort: the pity party!

As a member of a management team, you can quickly and effectively let your team know how upset you are by staging a breakdown. Phrases such as "I'm working so hard for you guys" or "I don't know what I'm doing wrong, I've done everything for you" or "I don't think you appreciate me" are all ways you can make your team feel guilty for their poor performance. Remember: guilt is every bit as effective as fear, so don't hesitate to use it. And like the old saying goes, "Never feel guilty for making people feel guilty—that defeats the purpose!"

Leading unpredictably and as emotionally as possible keeps people guessing, which is exactly where you want them to be. The more unstable you appear, the more likely they will pay attention to your every move. Now you have them right where you want them.

LET'S GET REAL

Great leadership means having a steady hand, steady heart, and steady mouth. There is no place in business (or in life for that matter) for leading through fear or guilt. These are manipulative tactics that will result in both broken people and a broken company. Every leader has moments of frustration, disappointment, and even anger. But your team is looking to you for calm resolve and focus on the issue, not emotional explosiveness. Putting your negative emotions on display will only do one of three things:

1. Give others permission to emulate your behavior.
2. Create a culture of fear that suppresses ideas and innovation.
3. And yes, send your employees running for the door.

This is not to say that you can't or shouldn't be open and authentic with your feelings. You can and should! But be impeccable with your words, your body language, and your tone. Be empathetic, and always come from a place of strength and calm resolve. Emotionally intelligent leaders are authentic and appropriate in their use of emotion. Stability from leadership produces stability in the workplace, and productivity is the result. Not to mention happiness, which is why people choose one workplace over another.

CHAPTER 11

SHOW UP AS ANYONE BUT YOURSELF

MY PERSONAL JOURNAL
Confidential
Tuesday, May 3

Today was horrible and I'm an absolute wreck. I'm exhausted and just about finished with this bottle of Chardonnay but I need to write anyway to get some stuff off my chest. I mean I guess it wasn't entirely horrible, I sure put on a good show—people still don't have a clue about this disaster of a divorce I'm going through ... thank God Jim's not being an ass about showing up to company events with me—we still look like the perfect, happy couple! And everybody still thinks we're the philanpthropists that we're not. He's not getting one dime and neither are his bogus charits that he "loves." ... The Xanax helps. I was able to sit through those boring strategy meetings all day AND go to that stupid charity function of his. I hate that charity and I hate those snot-nosed poor kids. Where do they come from anyway and why are there so many of them? Poor people just shouldn't have kids.

Sometimes I feel bad about not having kids but I don't like them and they don't like me. Why I ever started this lame company is beyond me other than it's been so easy to make a nonprofit look like a NONprofit. Suckers. I bet I can keep up the charade of making people think I can't have kids after they hear about the divorce. They'll think he left me because of that. How sad! Evil Jim leaves poor me, CEO of a K–12 Public Education Fund who can't even have her own children. Ha! Brilliant. The money will come pouring in—and I'll have to up my salary again, they can't say no now that I'm on my own financially, so there's that bonus. All right, well I feel better already—love journaling. Seems to be the only thing I tell people I do that I actually do. Gotta get to sleep—early morning showing up at the gym for coffee again. No one is the wiser that I don't work out before hitting the gym Starbucks. God, who has time for that. Besides, it's easier to stay this thin by not eating or by eating and barfing.

Note to self: call doc for a refill on the oxy, try "back pain" this time.

Are the public and private sides of you diverging more than usual? Sound familiar? If so, great job! Look, we're all human, and we all have the normal everyday life struggles to contend with, but like they say, "Don't let 'em see you sweat!" You'll hear all kinds of advice about being *authentic* or *genuine* or even that overused term *vulnerable*, but following advice like this will only expose your true weaknesses (if you actually have any), and that's just not good for your personal brand. It's certainly not real leadership.

You're the leader, and you need to give everyone around you the impression that you always have it together. You're smart and in charge, period. This isn't hard to do, but it's hard to be consistent about doing it. Flaws (inconsistencies) in your story lead to questions about your authenticity, and the biggest trick to being authentic is appearing to be authentic all the time. So here are a few tips and tricks to keep your story straight:

- Develop an image of how you want others to see you, and then be that person.
- Remember your lies and keep them consistent. Never ever deviate from your original story.
- Invest your energy in activities, friendships, and interests that make you look more interesting and more thoughtful than you are (you don't have time to be thoughtful).
- Pretend to care, and feign interest in things and people that bore you.
- Keep your actual personal life entirely to yourself.
- Never ever say, "I don't know."

No one really needs or wants to know your dirty laundry. It's dirty. The only reason people get caught up in scandals or fraud is because they talk too much. Don't try to explain away things that don't make sense or numbers that don't add up. Let someone else do that, and just keep repeating your standard stump speech. Eventually people will get tired and stop asking. If you ever actually do get caught with your pants down or your hand in the cookie jar, blame another person or a mental breakdown. Remember, it's never ever ever your fault. And, if they get too close to what is actually happening or to the manufactured truth, use the bright, shiny star tactic: "Look, over there!" Deflect, diffuse, confuse works every time. Do anything to get the attention away from the dirty laundry, which again, no one really wants to see.

LET'S GET REAL

Truth be told, authenticity (the real kind) is one of the most important values that a great leader can have. It's not a buzzword to be glossed over, taken lightly, or casually woven into the core values of a company. It's something that requires a lot of personal thought and exploration, maturity, security, and sense of self. Of course we're not proposing that you overshare details that compromise your privacy or constantly blather on about your problems. What we are proposing is that you accept the fact that you're human, and be the only human that you are at all times.

Companies often go through long, arduous processes of defining their company values without first doing the important work of defining the values of the people as individuals. Understanding your own values, and making them known to everyone you encounter through your actions (assuming of course that your values are good) is what good leadership is all about. Strong personal values and a moral compass that is pointing in the right direction are what allow you to be imperfect, to make mistakes, and to ask for help when you need it.

As the leader of any organization or group, you are the ethical compass. You have the fiduciary duty, whether real or implied, to operate honestly, ethically, and morally. If you don't, neither will anyone who works for you. There are not shades of the truth. There is not *truthiness* there is only *the truth*, and as a leader, you will know what that is.

It takes a lot of energy to keep up the charade. Keepin' it real takes none at all.

CHAPTER 12

DROP YOUR INTEGRITY

Remember to jot down what you said to Jen so you can practice it a couple of times when repeating it.
—BB

There is a lot of loose talk about integrity as a defining characteristic of a good leader. It's just not true. It's a bunch of BS and the word itself is significantly overrated. If you look at any astoundingly successful leader, it's not integrity that's gotten them all the promotions, raises, and accolades from countless employees and clients. In fact it's just the opposite!

When you look closely at successful leaders, the more they've said one thing and done the opposite, the more they win! Regularly dropping integrity has been a cornerstone of the meteoric rise of so many great leaders in the corporate world. The reason this works so well is that most people want to believe what you say, so it's pretty easy to fool them. The key is to remember what you've said to whom so you can back up your stories and keep track of them.

Dropping integrity can be a tricky when you're leading a team, so some stealth has to go into it. Let's say you know an idea is a dog and you want to use this to further your own career. Get the team together and explain that you want everyone to appear to be working on the project, but, because you are concerned about their careers, you don't want them to work too hard on it. You know it's going to fail but you want to protect all of them. They'll appreciate your sincerity and thank you for saving them from this loser of a project. Of course you don't really care about their careers, you just want to make sure that this thing sinks to the bottom of the bay faster than the *Titanic*. More importantly though, make sure you're not on it when it goes down. And if for some reason the damn thing floats to the top, you can blame the team for doing such a crappy job on it and fire a few of them for good measure. It's a win-win strategy for you and integrity didn't play any part in it.

Of course for this type of strategy to work in the long term, you will need allies, but you have to be very, very careful about whom you choose. Make sure it's someone with big ambition and no integrity as well. This can be a bit of a problem if you're trying to screw each other, so just make sure it's not a peer and always someone lower on the food chain than you. Someone in HR can be a good pick as they always have the dirt on the entire company, and with very little effort, you can almost always get it out of them. Ultimately, however, you have to be or at least act like you are better at this game than your ally. You have to be ready to drop your integrity at the first sign that the ally might be dropping theirs to screw you. You have to be ready to rat them out at the first sign they might be disloyal. This cannot be tolerated in anyone. Also, keeping rivals warring will serve you better in the long run. They never know who's screwing whom (sometimes literally). Do remember to keep notes or a journal or diary so you can remember what to use when you need it!

The higher than normal turnover will happen because you will have to fire anyone who has the temerity to question your integrity. Even if you have to make something up to fire them, the risks of keeping them are greater than a potential wrongful termination. Your truth can never be exposed. It's yours and for you alone to know. If indeed anyone figures out what you have done, remember: denial is not a river in Egypt, it's your first and last line of defense. Deny, deny, deny and blame someone else. Then act very hurt. Your basic lack-of-integrity defense strategy is deny, blame, feign hurt. Works every time! Look at all the leaders who have used this strategy and moved ahead in their careers! Unbelievable!

Of course, dropping your integrity can be used for all sorts of good. If the company is cash rich, figure out how you can use some, all in the name of business. Planning a trip to Italy with the family? Just figure out some client or business purpose why one of those days might be business, then expense the whole damn trip, first class of course, on the company. Seriously, you're having to interrupt your vacation to do business. It's the least the company can do. Oh, and be sure to put everything on one of your personal credit cards, then submit for reimbursement so you can get all those points! Even if the company frowns on it, you're in a leadership position, you do what you want. Don't ever let those damn bean counters try to shut you down. Fire their asses if they get too uppity. There are always more to fill that role.

Ultimately, there is no advantage to having integrity as a leader. It's just a stupid, chump move. And it's weak. Dropping your integrity for your own benefit is by far the harder move and takes more leadership skill. But the benefits far outweigh the downside. Be a leader, drop your integrity!

LET'S GET REAL

Regardless of what you read in the news about rich or successful leaders who regularly drop their integrity, it's not true. Their success is temporary. Their reputation as a cheater or liar is baked, and no amount of PR is ever going to cover up that ugly mess. They live in fear that someone is out to get them, and rightly so because of all the harm they have caused. You will also see those deceitful leaders who seem to defy logic, whose outright lies and outlandish, unethical behavior are jaw-dropping and there seem to be no consequences. Just wait, there will be. There are also those who will follow these leaders to the ends of the earth because these leaders have selectively tuned out all that does not fit their truth and have explained away the rest. This is called a cult. Sometime it takes awhile for them to be called out, but it always happens.

Integrity is yours. It's the calling card of good leadership and successful teams. Don't treat it lightly. Care for it and guard it with your life. You'll need it not only as a leader but as a person.

CHAPTER 13

BE LOVED

Sent: Tuesday, June 1 at 9:00 pm From: ME!
To: All Staff
Subject: Summer Picnic at MY HOUSE!

Hey guys!!!!!!!

In thinking about what we could do this summer to have some fun together, I wanted to suggest that we have a summer picnic at my house on Wednesday the 23rd. I know it's the middle of the week but you all totally deserve a break! Of course it will be a paid day, and I know production will have to stop for a day, but we can make it up by the end of the month don't ya think?! You guys should definitely invite your spouses and SO's! And kids too! I rented a giant bouncy house that they are just going to love. Let's not do a potluck, that's way too much work for you, I'll have it catered. I know I've been going on about our numbers being down, but you deserve it and I think it would be great for us all to throw back some beers and have a BBQ, and there are so many families I've never met and I really want to.

So let me know what you guys think! I'll send out a calendar invite later today and a map. If anyone needs a ride let me know, my house is about an hour from the office but I'm happy to come into town and pick a few people up. This is going to be so much fun! Should we get T-shirts??

Let's face it, we all need a little lovin' and leaders need more of it than most. Your job is stressful, you're faced with tough decisions, and you work harder than anyone, so you deserve to be showered with love and adoration. It's owed to you, so rake it up every chance you get. More often than not, the most superb leaders are forced to completely ignore their home and family life, which (while a sacrifice well worth making for the money) can result in a lack of love and admiration from spouses and children that must be made up for in some way. And there's no better place to turn than your work family in times like these.

Some methods for ensuring that you receive the love and adoration you so richly deserve and need are:

- Make sure that you are the head cheerleader and that everyone is having fun all the time. Give all of your people parties, picnics, team-building events, morale-building events, days off, snow days, perks, benefits, bonuses, raises, trophies, plaques, kudos, and hugs every day. Make your company the party bus that everyone wants to ride! These things are the hallmark of great leadership. The more you give, the more they take, and the more they love you.

- Make sure you construct your org chart so you can completely avoid delivering negative feedback to anyone. Being negative is not your job. Make it someone else's job to be despised and resented because you need your people's positive energy for your own personal stamina. Leadership can really suck it out of you, so you gotta fill it back up with someone else's energy from time to time.

- Don't exempt yourself from kudos and awards and the recognition you deserve; rather, guilt your people into giving you those things by playing the martyr card! Draw as much attention to yourself as possible by airing your personal problems, complaining, and feigning being overworked.

LET'S GET REAL

Great leaders don't need to be loved, they need to be liked and respected. Let's break this down with some definitions to make sure we're all on the same page.

Loving = Caring: Love is a complex word and a multidimensional emotion. In a broad sense, it is not traditionally used in describing professional matters. But one aspect of love that should be used in business is the aspect that means care. When leaders don't care for or about the people they work with, it shows. When employees don't care about the actual people who are their leaders, when they see a company's leadership simply as *corporate* or the *top brass* or *the powers that be*, it shows and has a direct and negative impact on company culture. A bidirectional sense of genuine caring leads to productivity, job satisfaction, retention, and for leaders, an enormous sense of purpose and reward. But some leaders need to be loved for a more self-serving purpose: as validation to bolster their self-esteem. An ongoing effort or campaign to be loved by your employees inhibits your ability to make decisions, and limits your ability to remain objective and fair. If the caring aspect of love is in play, your most difficult decisions will be respected, your employees will be more motivated to follow your guidance and help you when you need it, and your culture will flourish.

Admired = Respected: Let's not confuse adoration with admiration. You do not need to be adored by those you lead, but you should be admired. Admiration is born out of a sense of respect, and when you are respected, you are appreciated. Being appreciated as a leader is validating and an excellent boost for your self-esteem. Separating this from adoration ensures that you fulfill the need but maintain the space necessary to make good decisions and remain objective. But this is also a bidirectional imperative: ask yourself if you respect and admire the people you lead. If you don't, there is a systemic problem with your culture (or with you) that needs to be resolved swiftly. Because if you don't respect them, they definitely don't feel appreciated.

CHAPTER 14

MANAGING YOUR PERSONAL BRAND

Social Media got your head in a spin about managing your personal brand? We're here to help! Social media and personal brand management for leaders can be a daunting but important task. As a leader all eyes are on you, and how you present yourself on the Internet is job #1! Included in this chapter is a handy checklist of all of the social media sites where you should have a profile and account, as well as notes about how and what to post and how often to post. Blasting the interwebs with your messy digital footprint by garnering attention and followers will help drive your business forward, position you properly against your competition, and keep the buzz going about what events you're attending, the thought leadership you're contributing to your industry, and even what you're wearing!

Remember: all PR is good PR, so don't hold back. You've got a lot to say and a lot of people to say it to. In this chapter, we'll cover the basics of the some top social media platforms such as:

- LinkedIn
- Twitter
- Facebook
- Instagram
- Snapchat
- Tumblr
- Pinterest
- YouTube

LinkedIn: LinkedIn is social media for smart people, so it's important that you keep your profile updated and include all the relevant information about your career and accomplishments. But be yourself and don't fall into the trap of posting a stuffy corporate headshot. Post a photo that says something about who you are and what you like to do in your spare time. Perhaps a photo of you on your boat with a frosty gin and tonic, or a powerful image of your latest trip to the gun range. It's always refreshing to see authenticity! You should keep your eye on the feed and like, like, like posts from people you want to do business with or who have something you can gain from. Ignore the rest. Don't ever post any content of your own though. Your thought leadership is valuable and shouldn't be given away for free. And remember, LinkedIn is a social platform for smart people, so if you do feel compelled to post something original, make sure you copy it from something smart that's hard to find on Google.

Twitter: Twitter is the most popular social media platform frequented by celebrities, politicians, and important businesspeople like you. Use it liberally and don't hold back. Your fans want to see you as your true self. Using emojis, smart punctuation, and quippy 280-character statements can get you noticed, and using the right hashtag (#) can get you noticed in new circles. It's not the quality of your followers that's important, it's the quantity! So collect as many new followers as you can as quickly as you can by posting memorable images daily. Bathroom mirror selfies are a popular and quick method of letting the world know what you're up to and what you're thinking about yourself throughout the day. Twitter is also a wonderful place for you to go incognito by creating a fake account. This way you can troll your competitors, stalk your employees, and even pretend to be an adoring fan of your own brand! Who needs to create fake news when we can actually be fake people on Twitter!

Facebook: Facebook is a family-oriented social media site (and is frequented mostly by old people for whom Twitter is too complicated), so you will want to post pictures of yourself at home spending lots of time doing family things like cooking, throwing parties, binge drinking, and looking like you enjoy your kids. You should be *friends* with everyone on your staff as this is part of being authentic and your true self. Facebook is also a wonderful site to get to know your staff, what they like to do in their free time, where they live, and what kind of people they associate with. Often, your employees will post thoughts and ideas about their workplace—important stuff for you to read and stay up on! Posting at random times throughout the work day will send a clear message that it's OK for you to post on Facebook during the workday but not for them. Make notes about who is posting during the day and have your HR professional keep a daily log. These activities can be discussed at performance reviews.

Instagram: Instagram is a social media site for posting pictures of things you like such as artwork, places you've traveled, and food. It's a particularly convenient place to post entire albums of your last vacation or the vacation you are currently on, and is the ideal platform for creating a visual diary of your enviable life. Your staff will enjoy seeing that you are indeed spending your *think time* engaging in activities that will help drive your vision forward. The more cultural the better—if you're not able to post images from art galleries and museums, or if you're not able to cook visually appealing meals, you can always copy and paste something directly from the Internet and voilà! it looks like somewhere you visited or something you cooked yourself.

Snapchat: Remember Anthony's Weiner? Well, Snapchat is the Internet's answer to leaders accidentally posting or sending the wrong message publicly. Snapchat is an instant messaging platform that allows you to communicate in private (with photos!), and it automatically deletes your message once it's been read. It's perfect for sexting—an activity that you deserve to have fun with, but one that you definitely don't want falling into the hands of your employees or the public. It can also be used for sending instant messages to employees with whom you might be on the fringe of HR violations. If you're having an inter-office fling, stick with Snapchat for those late-night trysts.

Too busy for all this? Go ahead and pay someone else to post as you. Just make sure they are being authentic when they pretend to be you.

LET'S GET REAL

Personal brand is a tricky term. What it should mean is simply who you are, what you think, what your values are, and what you do. But in today's world, it can be used as a platform for developing a persona that is not you at all, but rather someone you want the world to think you are. Simply put, someone who doesn't exist. Personal brand management really should mean the ongoing effort to:

a. Ensure that everything published about you (by you or anyone else) is true, authentic, and genuine

a. Publish valuable thought leadership that is useful and informative to others

a. Use common sense and good judgment

The landscape of social media can be useful, but it can also be littered with landmines. Don't feel compelled to overuse it—to use platforms simply because your competitors or colleagues do—and, most importantly, don't buy into the idea that quantity trumps quality when it comes to who you engage with on these platforms. Your privacy is yours to protect, and your image is yours to preserve. Your reputation is yours and only yours to manage.

CHAPTER 15

EVIL RULES

Sent: Friday, August 31 at 11:46 pm
From: SVP Sales
To: CEO
Subject: Plan is in motion

The plans are in place and the information I've gathered over the last year or so should be helpful to you in the transition. I'm having difficulty with one of the SVPs as she might be getting suspicious, but as we've discussed she might be on the chopping block anyway.

I look forward to serving you in any way I can and as I'm sure you have noticed, I'm able to get information for you quite easily. Thanks for your consideration of my expertise and position in the new regime. Congratulations on putting it all together!

Sometimes leading the sheep to slaughter is so easy it's like taking candy from a baby. There is always a place for treachery, dirty deeds, and just plain evil in the workplace, but as a leader use those tactics if and only if doing so benefits you directly.

Another caution for all of you who think being an evil leader is easy and quick, it's not. The devil (pun intended) is in the details. Patience is required to be evil properly. You bide your time, lay the trap, and then smile from ear to ear when it catches your intended target.

Of course, if you're the leader, doing this is not really evil. It's just good leadership because it accomplishes a goal. Admittedly, it may be a completely selfish and narcissistic goal, but it's your goal so any means to that end will do. Let's take our butt-kissing SVP in the email for example. He was solely responsible for gathering intel on his coworkers while angling for a big promotion. He was evil, but his boss was an evil genius.

Once all the information had been gathered and the traps had been set, the CEO pulled a fast one on her little Judas. She let the SVP know that the one person he really wanted to see fired would be staying on and reporting to him. Naturally he was pissed, but as a student of the *evil tactic*, he saw the brilliance of his Machiavellian leader and decided to go with it and live to see another day. The CEO's move was classic evil—never let your Judas think they have the upper hand because of all the dirty deeds they may have accomplished. Create rivalries among all your evil-doing subordinates, then watch the magic that happens. You'll have more information, more competitiveness, and more people kissing your ass than you can shake a finger at. This is evil at its finest hour. Sit back and enjoy the scotch, knowing you won and you have scapegoats should any blowback come your way.

While patience is required to lead with evil, you also must focus on your purpose. Evil for evil's sake is just stupid. You must have a purpose or it will come back at you and ultimately not serve any purpose. Remember, all evil must be in the service of something and for you and you alone. Occasionally, you might engage in evil acts at the behest of others or for their benefit. Be careful in these cases, as you might lose control, and when using evil tactics, control is a necessity. Never leave anything to chance: play out all scenarios and make sure *you* are the beneficiary of any outcome.

Occasionally, there will be unintended consequences. The key here is to make sure you've set yourself up for total deniability and have someone to blame. If you don't, you're a weak leader and you have only yourself to blame. Shame on you! Evil is a tool to be used only by the most skilled of leaders. What made you think you were worthy? You don't get to this level of leadership by being weak. There's no crying when using evil. If you're not ready to kill or be killed, this is not a leadership characteristic for you. Go back to leadership day care.

LET'S GET REAL

Evil never wins in the end. You might win a battle or two by being a complete douchebag like the characters in this story, but ultimately you lose as leader. Your team will never respect you; they may fear you, but respect will never come. They'll make fun of you behind your back, they'll never tell you the truth, and they won't help you succeed.

You might be tempted to get even or show up someone who has been particularly evil in the workplace. Resist the temptation. Once you go down that road, your reputation will follow. One wrong act will likely lead to another. Own the first one, apologize, make everyone whole, and don't do it again. Don't be an asshole; be fair and be truthful.

CHAPTER 16

TEARS: YOUR POWER DRUG

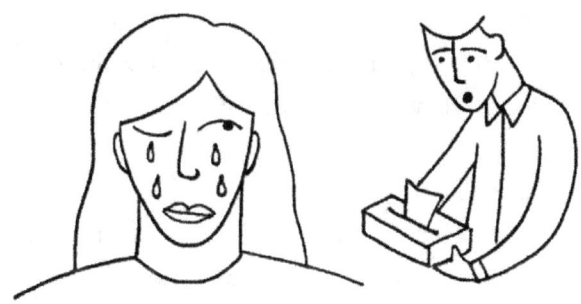

Sent: Friday, August 26 at 4:49 pm
From: CEO
To: Executive Team
Subject: Recent Feedback—Mandatory Meeting

Meet me in the conference room at 5:00 to discuss the conversations I've overheard all of you having about me. I'm not happy.

Whether you're a woman or a man, tears are your friend. Not so if you're some peon at the lower rungs of the corporate ladder, but if you're large and in charge, tears are truly your secret weapon.

Tears can be used so effectively and manipulatively that no one will ever catch on. When someone cries, most people feel the need to provide some kind of comfort or relief. The truth is they're secretly glad they're not the one crying, so everyone puts on a public show of sympathy. You want to use this phenomenon to your advantage.

If you're having trouble getting your team to come around to your point of view or if someone doubts your intentions (there may be a good reason for it, but let's not dwell on that), just begin to look down and cover your eyes ever so modestly. Don't say anything; let the silence do the heavy lifting. Then when you've worked up a good tear or two, slowly lift your head so they can see your red-rimmed baby blues. Once you've spotted the sympathy on their faces, you're on! It's show time, baby!

Keep silent for a few more minutes so it really sinks in that you're hurt, then do the best that you can to fake genuine pain, and ask why anyone would question your integrity (remembering, of course, that it didn't have anything to do with your integrity, but you need to act as if it did). This will catch your audience totally off guard. Now you have the complete upper hand, so go in for the kill. Say something like, "I know what you've been saying behind my back about this, so go ahead and tell me to my face. I can take it." Your opposition will be so dumbfounded, they will completely forget why they disagreed with you in the first place. Of course, you didn't really hear what was being said behind your back because you just made that up, but you need to act as if you did to make this believable. They probably won't say anything because they have no idea what you're talking about. If, by chance, they do relay some gossip about you, so much the better. In either case, just look them directly in the eye and say, "I'm surprised by you and very disappointed and deeply ... hurt." (Pause and take a breath before you say *hurt*.) This always gets them and the rest of the team will be stunned, hoping you don't look in their direction next. They all know they've dissed you at some point and are deathly afraid you really do know what they said. Step one of mission accomplished.

Now for the coupe de grace: say, "I'm really disappointed in all of you. I had one simple idea I was trying to get through that would benefit all of you, and this is the reward I get. I'm deeply and profoundly hurt." Bingo! You will now get buy-in from the whole team for whatever you want. The biggest ass kisser in the room will suck up first and say he is so sorry and of course he supports you. One by one, they will all fall in line and presto changeo! you win. See how easy that was? Tears are the magic elixir.

Another way to really use tears to your advantage is when you're faking passion about something. Tears are great at big gatherings when you're on stage to make a point about how passion ate you are. Strategically stop midsentence as if you're choked up, so that you have the sympathy of the whole audience, and then tell them why you believe so passionately about whatever you are blathering on about. Touch your chest a few times, dab your eye once or twice; you'll have them eating out of the palm of your hand.

This is even more effective for a man because, when a guy cries we all stop and take a tenderhearted breath. Wow, this must be serious, and look how vulnerable he is? So listen, guys, work it; tears can be your best friend too.

Bottom line, tears are the ultimate tool to get your way. No one can say no to a crying boss, even if it's completely ginned up! And they will love your *sincerity*, which is really the kicker.

LET'S GET REAL

Never ever use tears or theatrics to manipulate people, it's a form of emotional abuse. Human beings are wired to have sympathy for others in pain, so when it appears as if someone is in pain, we automatically give up our own agenda for theirs. When authentic, this is an act of compassion and probably why we've survived as a species. But when used as a manipulative tactic, it's more than painful: it's painfully obvious.

Be real and be authentic. If you need to cry, do so, but if you're doing it in public make sure people know why. If you're upset about something from home and it bleeds into the workplace, say so. Don't let people assume that you're upset with them or with work. Ultimately, crying is not something you want to do on a regular basis; it's just not useful at work. If a situation warrants a genuine cry, whether you're male or female, it can be powerful. But, if used inauthentically, crying will leave you powerless.

SECTION 3

LEADING BY EXAMPLE

Introduction
THE ROAD TO HELL, PERFECTLY PAVED BY YOU

Sadly, there are probably more examples of bad leadership than good in the world. Once you've been given the leadership reins, it's up to you to constantly ask yourself if you are heading down the path of good (great is even better) leadership. Never make the assumption that you are a good leader; you always have to analyze and validate the results of your leadership. But don't worry, the results of your leadership are easy to spot if you know where to look: directly at the people around you. If they are emulating good leadership they will be productive, happy, and collaborative, leading and mentoring others. If they are emulating bad leadership, you will see a broken culture, attrition, gossip, confusion, and ultimately poor company performance.

The first thing some new leaders do is try to be best friends with everyone in the hopes that, if they like you, they'll do what you want and make you look good. Nope! This almost always backfires because eventually you have to tell your people something they don't like and just like that, you're the boss. Or what they're really thinking is, "What a jerk!"

Another leadership newbie strategy is to micromanage the living daylights out of everyone to make sure things are being done *right* (code for *my way*). This is quickly followed by other common forms of leading by example such as shaming and bullying. These didn't work that well when you were in grade school, and guess what, adults really don't like to be shamed or bullied either. Moreover, they're not only ineffective, they're dangerous.

If you think that keeping everyone in the dark about what you're really doing and playing the game of saying different things to different people is going to keep them on their toes and always trying to please you, you're painfully mistaken. Leading this way spreads dissent and gossip, neither of which ever moves the needle forward. And yes, it makes you look like a jerk ... again. If you've been leading this way, you're probably getting desperate. So what do you do? Abdicate. Just ignore it all and hope it gets done right. Don't listen and then place the blame on everyone but the person staring back at you in the mirror.

So here's some sound advice for potential leaders when their leadership lottery number comes up: mentor, mentor, mentor. Human beings love to learn and will learn if you're patient. That means figuring out what they want to learn and what resources they need, and then working with them to get there. Point them to your examples and the examples of others. Answer questions and be available. Focus on results, grounded in the values of the organization, and let them figure out what process works best for them. Your way is only one way, not necessarily their way or the best way.

Know that as a leader, you are being watched every moment. In all you say and all you do. Your position is like being in the house of mirrors at the carnival: you can run but you can't hide. What do you want your people to see? A human being who is authentic, does their best, cares about the mission as much as the team, and provides a training ground for future leaders to learn by example.

Leadership is not only about positive results for your company, it's about positive results for everyone you encounter as well as for yourself. The example you set with your good leadership transcends your immediate team and environment: it will be judged by your customers, your industry, your peers, and yes, your friends and family. You have both an amazing opportunity and a heavy responsibility to set a good example through your actions, your words, and the promises you make. It's on you.

CHAPTER 17

MICROMANAGE THE SHIT OUT OF EVERYTHING

Sent: Sunday, August 15 at 8:50 pm
From: CEO
To: Executive Team
Subject: Daily Reports

I continue to be dismayed by your daily reports, they are lacking in the level of detail that I specifically asked for. I want no deviation or interpretation from my written instructions. These are critical to my insight into the work you are supposed to be doing. Some of you are not using the template I asked you to, so you'll need to redo the reports from the last couple of months. I want them to be consistent.

All of them.

I look forward to seeing your revisions tomorrow.

Thanks.

One of the keys to great leadership is to get in and pull up the plants so you can examine the roots. Sure, occasionally you will cause the plant to die, but more often than not, you'll catch root rot early.

You must always know everything that happens in your company, because if you don't, bad things will happen. You can't really trust your people unless you know exactly what they're doing every step of the way. Of course, this can become problematic as your organization grows, so you have to essentially clone yourself with others who are equally diligent and detailed.

To make sure that you have supreme and all-encompassing knowledge of the organization and your people, start with your leadership team. Only hire those who are absolutely loyal to you and have shown that loyalty by following your instructions to the tee: no deviation, no ideas of their own, no questions. They are obedient, observant, and loyal soldiers to you first and to the organization second. Even one breach of this protocol should be cause for termination.

Once you have established that you have dutiful soldiers on your leadership team, you need to make it explicitly clear that every detail, no matter how small, is worthy of your attention. And, by extension, their attention. However, you don't want to hear about it; you want detailed written reports. Not that you'll read them all. The purpose is for your people to provide them so you know they have eyes on everything. It's about control. The more you micromanage your people, the more control you will have. And the more secure they will feel.

Now you might be saying that this will take a lot of time. And you're right, it does. But if people aren't reporting on everything they're doing, how will anyone know what's going on? Remember that people can't really be trusted to do their jobs without supervision. They just don't know any better. By requiring over reporting on everything they're doing, you keep them doing the work, reporting on the work, and learning a lot about the right way to do things! In the end micromanaging is really for them as well.

Occasionally you'll encounter someone who questions the reporting requirements. This person needs to go. It's not about the report, it's about the reporting process, so they really learn what they're doing. Don't defend yourself. That is unworthy of you, and the person who questioned you obviously doesn't know about good leadership.

Micromanaging is also a great way to ensure that nothing changes, that your way (the right way) is always followed. There is great accomplishment in exactitude, and you want to make sure not only that your outcome is achieved but that the way you want it done is followed as well. You do not want change as this leads to chaos, and chaos is a challenge to your leadership.

So go ahead, pull up the plants to inspect the roots all you want. It works. Teach your team to do the same, and before long, you'll have a well-oiled machine that is doing exactly the same thing all the time. Success will be yours. Employees really love this too as it teaches them discipline and obedience, exactly what they need to be successful under your leadership.

LET'S GET REAL

Micromanaging anything or anyone is a recipe for failure. Almost everyone has been at the mercy of the kind of manager who is so insecure that they need to inspect and direct your every move. The result is always the same: a completely disempowered work force that is dying on the vine and eventually leaves because a low-tech robot could do their job.

When first working with a manager, you'll need to pay more attention than you will after they start learning the work. Intervene early and often, then let them go. Innovation and ideas come from them figuring out problems on their own.

Micromanagement stifles innovation every single time. You should keep your attention on the results, not how they got there.

Endless, pointless reports? Get rid of them. Focus on the results and forget about the process as long as it's working. No one likes documenting things that are already easily discernible. And everyone realizes this is a form of control, so use reports that actually tell you something and ditch the rest.

CHAPTER 18

BE BEST BUDS

Sent: Wednesday, October 18 at 11:29 am
From: Suzanne, VP Global Sales To: John, Regional Sales Associate
Subject: Lunch? And Ouch!

Hey there,

How were your morning sessions? Mine were boring. This conference is a bust. Do you wanna skip the luncheon and just go out and get lunch on our own? At least this thing is in a fun city. But man, those margaritas last night were killers. I had a massive hangover through most of the speakers this morning. As usual you were hilarious John … and I promise I won't tell anyone about your choice of karaoke song if you don't tell anyone about my missing shoe! Ha ha ha! Total walk of shame this morning through the hotel though, seems that guy didn't mind a little overtime with the one-shoed chick.

By the way, I can't have dinner tonight, I have to work on your review because I blew it off last night. It's due to the C.E. "HO" by Monday.

She's such a skank I hate her.

Me

This is the kind of special bond that makes an employee/employer relationship last. Not only is it an example of getting on the same level and seeing eye to eye with your direct reports, it shows that you're human, just looking to have a good time like everyone else.

It's true that it's lonely at the top. When you're a great leader, people distance themselves from you because they don't feel like they're on the same level as you. If you're really effective, they will even fear you. But great leaders need friends just like everyone else, so there's no reason not to reach out and forge a few of those friendships yourself. Bonds and friendships in the workplace can also offer you inside information from the desk-level workforce. Once you have their trust, they can tell you where to find performance problems, give you a better sense of the culture you're creating, and best of all, help prop up your confidence by reminding you how great you are and how much everyone adores you.

Business travel is the most effective method for creating some of these bonds. When scheduling business travel, be mindful of who will be joining you on the trip and use this opportunity to create lasting memories and tight bonds with a special employee who you already think highly of or are attracted to. Sharing a *what happens on the road stays on the road experience* with a subordinate is a sure-fire way of creating a bond that will result in a lasting friendship and give you an outlet for sharing details about your personal life that you wouldn't be able to share with just any employee. And hey, you only live once, so if it feels good in the moment, don't hold back. Once they realize that you have bestowed the gift of friendship and your most intimate secrets (or more!) upon them, they will be even more loyal to you and a better steward of your vision throughout the organization.

Remember, no one is immune to top down scrutiny, so when

the heat's on you from above, it's important for your boss to see how much your team adores you. In the workplace, intimacy is hands down the best currency with which to buy loyalty!

LET'S GET REAL

Do not confuse stupidity with authenticity. Yes, leaders should be accessible, approachable, and authentic, but if you are in a leadership position, you should show some self-respect and self-restraint when it comes to developing intimate friendships and relationships in the workplace.

Creating healthy boundaries for yourself and making them known through your actions doesn't create distance between you and your employees, it creates the space you need to remain objective. You can be friendly without being *friends* in the traditional sense and certainly without exchanging knowledge or information that compromises the organization or damages your credibility. You can also be familiar and fun without being *one of the gang* by appreciating that those friendships do and should exist in the workplace, they just shouldn't exist with you.

When you buddy up to an employee, single someone out, and put your special rapport with them on display, it may satisfy your need to feel liked, to feel relevant, to feel wanted, but it puts them in a terribly awkward situation with both you and their peers. With you, they no longer have the space they need to challenge you, to earn your respect, or even to enjoy a genuine sense of success when recognized for their achievements. Recognition is one of the best drivers of productivity, but only when it's recognition for the right reasons. With their peers, the results can be even more catastrophic when they are labeled a suck-up, which they undoubtedly will be thanks to you

So be friendly, but find your own friends.

CHAPTER 19

FOLLOW THE LEADER

Sent: Tuesday, July 25 at 11:30
From: CEO
To: Executive Team
Subject: Best Practices

Attached is the most lovely note that I received from a valued client after our award ceremony the other night. I honestly was not expecting the award at all (especially at my own company event—you guys are too much, thank you!) let alone this gracious note.

It goes to show you how important hand-written notes and personal gestures are. I'm glad I took the time to send them and I hope you do to. I expect you to learn from this example.

Sharing your insights with the team is important. Of course it doesn't always mean that they will follow them, but you have to try or at least give the impression that you are trying. You can't help it if some of them are rather dim and don't get it.

But, in the event that you have a few lemmings who can actually learn from your example, it's tactics like these that need to be shared and emulated. After all, duplicity multiplies and then you're doing more with much less!

As an example, when attending events that are in your honor (as they should be, if you're attending), make sure that you follow up thoughtfully. While you don't have time to be thoughtful, there must be someone on your staff who can help you appear thoughtful at all times. One way to accomplish this is to have your assistant write hand-written thank you notes, sign your name, and send them off in a timely manner. You might be surprised by the heart-warming response you get in turn—notes of gratitude for your gratitude and exemplary leadership and thoughtfulness. How this was executed is not the point. Like they say, "It's the thought that counts," and it was your idea, so there you go.

Make sure to get your whole team together when something like this happens, never let them get out of learning from your excellent example of leadership. It's important to give everyone a very detailed account of how you did this and why it succeeded. It's also important to set a new precedent and require that your people do what you did.

Your values and integrity should always be on display for others to emulate—including the tactics you use to display them. If this means shortcuts, leveraging the talents of others, taking credit for results generated from the innovation of others, or just appearing to be more thoughtful or resourceful than you actually are, share these tactics! Everyone will benefit from your knowledge and wisdom. And don't be stingy with that amazing assistant of yours—everyone should experience the value of personal administrative support and should all have access to it. He or she will simply have to understand that they are new to the game, and the charades just go with the internship.

LET'S GET REAL

It's as true as it is timeless: Great leaders lead by example. The upside of a leader who sets a good example is that, when the values he or she lives are right and good, they are multiplied and amplified so powerfully that an organization's brand can become known for its values. And not surprisingly, when a leader leads by example with values that lack integrity or honesty or that are just downright awful, the result is exactly the same: an amplification and multiplication of that same despicable behavior runs rampant throughout the organization, damages the brand, and becomes a firewall keeping good people and talent at bay.

Leadership is infectious, in both the most positive and potentially disastrous ways imaginable. It's your job as a leader to make sure that you lead by the kind of behavior you want to permeate your organization and out into the marketplace. As the leader you are the keeper, the steward, the guardian, and the master of those values, so make sure you live them every day in every way.

CHAPTER 20

THE WAITING GAME

Be right there—taking longer than I thought.

Just got into a fender bender. Cops taking for-EVER to write the report.

I threw my back out again, going to have to WFH. Can someone send me all the docs to review?

Slight emergency, gotta run to the vet.

Forgot my password, I can't login and nobody in IT is calling me back so I won't have feedback for you until tomorrow.

I'm going to be late for the Board meeting—tell them I'm meeting with a customer.

Bad day. Not going to make it by 10. Start without me, but you'll need to clear your schedules to stay late so you can catch me up on what I missed.

The conference call access code didn't work for me. What did I miss?

I thought the meeting was on Tuesday. I'm still at my beach house.

Postpone.

I'm out of time, it's just going to have to wait.

Be there in 10.

On my way.

Be there in 20.

That's exactly right: your schedule comes first, and don't let them forget it! Great leadership means making sure that those you lead are respectful of you and your schedule. Understanding and accepting that your schedule is the schedule that dictates theirs is their first step in a successful relationship with you. Make this known from the outset, and you will avoid conflict in the future. Not only is there the simple fact that you are busier than anyone else, there are also specific strategic reasons to operate on your own time and to never feel guilty about making them wait. Don't accept accusations of being disorganized or rude. Own your lateness and make it work. Here's how:

> **Make an entrance.** The more important the event or meeting is, the more grand your late entrance should be. This is an opportunity to make a statement about your importance, disrupt the meeting, and get everyone on their toes where they should be! When you enter a meeting in progress, make sure that your hands are full so that someone has to hop up and open the door for you, clear

a place for you at the head of the table, and help you with your belongings. This physical manifestation of subservience is a sure-fire way to start the meeting off right—it's just starting after all because you've just arrived. Having a coffee in hand is a great way to say, "I took my time getting here" without having to say a word. Holding the remains of a muffin or sandwich says, "This meeting is inconvenient for me and interrupts my flow." Showing up late in your gym clothes says, "I take care of myself first." And walking into a meeting while wrapping up a call on your cell is the ultimate way of letting everyone know how very, very busy and important you are.

Be indifferent. You do not have time to care or even notice what affect your tardiness or absenteeism has on those you lead. It's simply not your problem. The second you appear to care or be defensive about it, they will begin to manipulate you, and before you know it, you will be a slave to your team—not a dynamic of great leadership. So rise above the criticism they might level at you, and ignore them entirely. The only conversation that matters is how they are going to start marching to the beat of your drum.

Never apologize. You can't be indifferent if you're defensive or apologetic. Never ever apologize for missing an event or call or being late to a meeting. It's not your fault, it's just the way it is, and they have to adapt. You're the leader; your schedule is the schedule from which all else flows, and the more you put this into practice, the better for everyone. For that matter, never apologize about anything as a leader—it's weak and for losers.

Save your energy and adopt a scapegoat. If being indifferent or not apologizing is a challenge for you, then the right solution for you is to have a scapegoat. An executive assistant saves you energy by making your excuses for you, while also giving you someone to lay the blame on for your disorganization, lack of respect, and general thoughtlessness. Of course, your assistant should care or appear to care, and should be an excellent apologist taking full responsibility for your tardiness and absenteeism. If not, fire them now.

Remember: It's all about you, and practice makes perfect.

LET'S GET REAL

As a leader, the Golden Rule applies to you more than anyone. Your actions and words set the tone for your entire organization, so when you are disrespectful and inconsiderate of others, this behavior will be mimicked. Your entire culture will suffer, and before you know it, you will be sitting alone in that conference room while your people play the waiting game right back at you. The intentional culture you want starts with your actions, your behavior, and the values you demonstrate daily. Disrespect others and they will disrespect you. Every child knows this!

Nobody is ever too busy to be considerate. Consideration is not a factor of time, its a factor of respect. If your busyness causes you to be chronically late, then you need to take a good hard look at your inability to organize and prioritize, and get some help. Others are dependent on your leadership in order to reach their own goals, make their own deadlines, and manage their own workflow. Inconsistencies and lack of reliability on your part makes their jobs infinitely harder. No one will respect you or your time if you don't start by respecting their time.

So get it together: be on time, every time.

CHAPTER 21

WINNING THE BLAME GAME

Sent: Friday, October 18 at 5:45 am
From: VP Operations
To: CEO
Subject: Production Schedule Behind

Mark,

We have a huge problem with the production schedule.

It's 6 weeks behind and we're at risk of not getting the product to market in time for the holidays. I told Tom a month ago that he needed to step it up and start creating overtime schedules for his team so this wouldn't happen. Now finance is saying that they wouldn't approve the overtime because we don't have the funds, but nobody on that team told me at the time. Max's situation with his unhappy development team doesn't help matters. They hate him, productivity is suffering, and he's not doing anything about it. Sue is a basket case, she missed 4 days last month because of a sick kid or something and didn't hire the people we needed in Q2. To make matters worse, customer service has a massive backlog again—I was totally unaware of this until today. The whole thing is just a mess.

Leadership is about holding others accountable and not holding back when it comes time to call out others who aren't pulling their weight. The best way to not end up holding the bag is to have a constant eye on your peers and make sure that your superiors know exactly where to lay the blame when things go sideways. Make sure that those beneath you never blame you. Sometimes you must give everyone insight when others' poor performance isn't so obvious, and sometimes you might even need to inflate the story to make sure the responsibility is deflected away from you.

The more you focus on blaming, and the more detailed you can be in your accounts of where to lay that blame, the more confusing it will become for those you are making your case to. This is a good thing! Just keep piling it on in a never-ending stream of crafty storytelling sprinkled with somewhat truthful accounts of this and that injustice. The more you stay at it, the more solid the perception of your lack of responsibility will be.

As a leader, it's important to recognize and accept the fact that you are surrounded by incompetence. Laziness, apathy, distraction, stupidity, low energy, lack of stamina, lying, failure, general loserness, ugliness, and weakness is everywhere you look. You should always be looking for incompetence, and when you find it, point it out loudly and with complete conviction and confidence. One of the most valuable qualities in a good leader is awareness, including self-awareness, of the fact that you didn't get to where you are by being responsible for anything failure related. You got here by being responsible for success only. And that which is perceived as failure is actually success because if it hadn't failed like you intended it to, it wouldn't have been be so successful. Or something like that.

Let others worry about the view from under the bus. You're too busy driving it.

LET'S GET REAL

A cornerstone of great leadership is accountability and taking responsibility for yourself first and foremost. Blaming others is not only poor leadership, it has little if nothing to do with a solution to a problem. When people state the problem but offer nothing in the way of a solution, the only thing they are solving is how to take the focus off of themselves and project it onto others.

At the same time, some good leaders take too much of the blame for the shortcomings of others. Where did I go wrong? What could I have done differently? How did I let them down? While doing some of this kind of self-reflection is an important exercise in order to learn and improve, doing too much of it is simply not assigning accountability to those to whom it should be assigned. Be cautious with accountability—there is a fine line between ownership and blame. Awareness and a constant monitoring of this ebb and flow will help you both learn and teach.

We will always have performance problems with ourselves, with our peers, and with those we lead. But as leaders, those are the problems we're employed to solve. If we're unable to solve them, then we ourselves are the performance problem.

There are no winners in the blame game, because only losers play. As Arnold H. Glasow said, "A good leader takes a little more than his share of the blame, a little less than his share of the credit."

CHAPTER 22

HAZING AS AN ART FORM

Sent: Sunday, April 2 at 9:49 pm
From: CEO
To: Management Team
Subject: Performance Transparency

Team,

Let's face it, we've got a performance problem on our team. I'd like to see a stack ranking of all the PMs based on the amount of Q2 revenue they've managed and their respective gross margins. Once we have that, I'd like to call a meeting, get them all in a room, and put some feet to the fire. The slackers need to know who's carrying their weight and the performers need to be publicly rewarded for their hard work and accomplishments. I don't have a problem sending this report to allstaff@ either so let's plan on doing that directly after the meeting.

This is a business, not summer camp. And you are the leader, responsible for inspiration and positive motivation, but also for administering the smackdown when it's required. Peak performance means cracking the whip every now and again, so if you have to do it, do it right and do it hard.

Great leaders are masters of discipline and obedience. Oftentimes this means making your authority and your expectations crystal clear. Not only do you need to lead by example, you need to make examples of those who are not taking your leadership and your requirements seriously. There should be nowhere in your organization to hide and nowhere to run when the going gets tough.

There are many proven techniques and methodologies when the situation requires the reset of performance standards. Stack ranking is an effective way to let everyone know who the performance winners and losers are. The people on the top of the stack will be seen as exemplary performers, respected and revered. The people on the bottom of the stack will be seen as slackers and *the bag to drag* for others. This will cause a tribal phenomenon known as *corporacide*—a cost effective and swift method for making room for new talent.

Three-hundred-sixty-degree anonymous feedback is also an effective way to publicize humiliation and shame that are deserved for lack of performance. Being anonymous in nature, it allows for brutally honest feedback, which is often needed by those too clueless to recognize their own laziness or ineffectiveness. Peak performers need to vent their frustration with their coworkers, and anonymous feedback is a fantastic way to accomplish your mission for both the giver and the receiver of the feedback.

Leadership means sometimes it's going to hurt them a lot more than it's going to hurt you. So be swift, decisive, and make every whack count.

LET'S GET REAL

Kiss your culture goodbye if you resort to shame, humiliation, or bullying. Bullying and abuse do nothing but degrade and debase your employees, and not only are they wrong and unethical, they are downright dangerous. These practices can inflict lasting emotional damage to those who are subjected to them as well as those who are forced to administer them. They can cause permanent damage to personal confidence while derailing careers. In the worst cases, they can incite violence, retribution, and self-harm.

As a leader, you are 100 percent responsible for the safety and well-being of your employees at all times. Ensuring that abuse is not happening anywhere in your organization is on you. If it happens below you, deal with it immediately by terminating the abusers. If it happens above you, report it to your state's department of labor immediately, and include specifics.

Bullying happens in the workplace at a much higher rate than most of us realize. The Workplace Bullying Institute (WBI) defines bullying as "repeated mistreatment: sabotage by others that prevented work from getting done, verbal abuse, threatening conduct, intimidation, and humiliation". Just the fact that the WBI exists should be troubling enough for most employers and employees alike. And to prove the point, 2010 poll conducted by Zogby International for WBI showed that fully 37% of the total US workforce had been bullied at work. What's even more frightening is that an additional WBI report showed that 52% of time employees reported that employers did nothing to stop the bullying.[1]

---

[1]. Brown, "3 Ways to Kill Your Company's Idea Stifling Shame Culture," *Fast Company*, September 13, 2012, https://www.fastcompany. com/3001239/3-ways-kill-your-companys-Brené idea-stifling-shame-culture.

CHAPTER 23

GENDER MATTERS

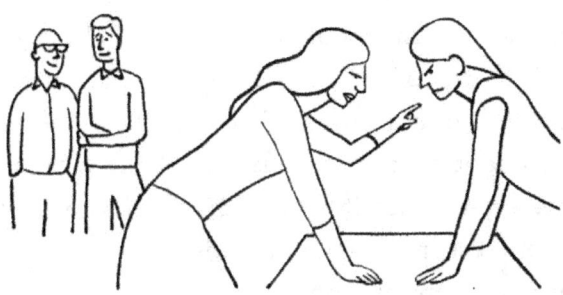

Sent: Wednesday, May 3 at 10:00 am
From: Christine To: Matt L.
Subject: Strategic Plan Due Soon ...

Hi there Matt,

Hey buddy! I wanted to give you a gentle nudge that your Q1 plan is due to me soon. The original deadline was Friday but I know you've been a busy guy so how about you try to get it to me by next Wednesday? Does that work for you? I really feel for you with all the pressure you've been under, you sure are handling it like a champ. As usual! ;)

Let me know if you need even more time. If you do, I can figure something out on my end. Hope to see you today, been missing having you around since you've been working from home more. If you need help, let me know, I'm happy to swing by your house one evening after work—I'll bring the wine!

Hugs,

Christine

Sent: Wednesday, May 3 at 10:02 am
From: Christine
To: Janice
Subject: Your Strategic Plan is Late
Get it to me by the end of the day. C.

When leading, employ the personality and style that are required for the situation. When dealing with men and women, it's completely okay to treat them differently. This is just good, solid leadership. Adapting to the situation. Being a versatile leader with chameleon-like qualities is admired and revered. Don't let any nerdy HR person tell you otherwise.

Woman to woman: Woman to woman management needs to be firm, direct, and devoid of any kind of emotion whatsoever. This is your best defense mechanism against what will forever be true: women are bitches! They are not going to like being managed by you simply because you are a woman, so meet them head on in the bitchscape of the professional environment and you'll avoid a lot of trouble. Plus, you know they want your job, so never let them see you sweat and always watch your back.

Woman to man: Get creative here ladies. Use all God gave you to get what you want. Dress appropriately when asking a male superior or subordinate for something. If you've got the gams, show 'em! If you've got a full rack, let it shine! Don't cover up your gifts in some bulky, work-appropriate attire. That's not how leaders dress. Make them think there is more package to be opened if only you get what you want. Who made the rule that trading sex for promotions is off limits? It's what leaders do. Lead them on, play the game, and above all else, use your sexuality to work the room and the situation.

Man to woman: This is fun, isn't it boys? You get to play hide the pickle with no consequence, assuming that the woman in front of you really wants something. If men were meant to ignore women's sexuality, all men would all be eunuchs, and we know that's not the case. So get in the game. Depending upon how good looking the woman is and what she wants, make her pay. It's a game of cat and mouse, and you're a dirty tomcat. If she lets you catch her, she's in the game too so no harm, no foul. And by the way, it's perfectly okay to make any woman that works for you your work wife. Every good male leader needs one.

Man to man: This is the most boring. Just treat him like any Joe Blow off the street. Unlike women, guys have few feelings, so you're not going to step on them. If you tell him to go to hell, depending upon his rank, he probably will. If it's a superior, kiss his ass, literally. They love it.

LET'S GET REAL

Good leaders do not use their gender or sexuality to get what they want. Male or female, they use their natural talents to move the organization or mission forward, regardless of gender. They respect everything that each person brings to the table, and they leverage it appropriately.

Unfortunately, there is a double standard in business today: many women leaders are parroting the sexist behavior of the men they despise. These lady leaders, usually the loudest and most annoying critics of male sexist behavior, are engaging in it themselves in the exact same way: doting on male employees, softening their message or their tone, and extending preferential treatment to that hot, hunky middle manager while silently and brutally attacking his female counterpart through intimidation, fear, and downright nastiness.

Let's be clear: we're not suggesting that you deny the fact that men and women are different, possess different natural skills, and engage in different communication styles. Not recognizing this fact very well may be the overcompensation that has lead to the oh-so-slow rise of women in leadership. Women will never be men and men will never be women, and struggling to treat them in the exact same way may stifle both parties' true potential.

If you are a woman leader, introducing your gender into the mix in a way that is manipulative or as obvious as Christine's blunders in the emails above is sexist at best, and it is as demeaning to men as Don Draper's attitude is to women. The salt in the wound is then assuming the role of Queen Bitch with your female employees. By showing them your icy side, you're only asking for the same (and most likely worse) ice storm to come your way.

Gender matters because gender diversity in the workplace is one of our greatest opportunities to have a strong, 360 degree approach to strategy, customer insight, and people management. But be smart and leave your insecure self behind.

CHAPTER 24

HUB AND SPOKIN'

Sent: Monday, July 24 at 9:30 am
From: CEO
To: Executive Team
Subject: One-to-Ones Today

I've got some critical information to share with each of you so starting at 11:00. I'll make myself available for individual meetings. Please just sign up with my assistant. I'll need 30 minutes with each of you. Clear your schedule to fit mine if you've already got something going.

All the leadership books tell you that, in order to grow a great team, you need to mentor people. Naturally, you might have found mentoring to be a strong suit of yours as people always gravitate towards you as a leader and want to learn from you. The key to mentee development is to meet individually with each of your team members. You're probably thinking, "Geez, doesn't that take up a lot of time?" Not if you do it the right way!

Only do it once a month. That's plenty of time for you to get your point across. These meetings are called one-to-ones, but it's Hub and Spokin' really your time to ascertain whether or not this person is being loyal to you. Not to the company, only to you. Of course, you will impart some words of wisdom, but if they don't respond with a sufficient level of praise and gratitude, you might have a problem. Naturally, you'll want to tell them it's all about them and you are there to listen, but seriously, what could they possibly say that you don't already know—or should know!

So, here's the real brilliance of mentoring. Call it hub and spokin,' a takeoff on some speaker somewhere who talked about culture. Bottom line, you're the hub, always because, as the hub, you're the greatest person in the room and everyone else is well, less than that. If you want to keep your team in line, you have to be the repository of all information, and you get to decide who hears what. Whether it's the same information you're sharing with each of them, or different information, the important thing is to do it separately! This way you maximize your pull. If your people all hear the same thing at the same time, you run the risk of them ganging up on you because you've lost your leverage! The key is keeping them isolated and guessing.

Don't bother to set these as recurring meetings, because, Gawd, that would really play havoc with your schedule, and you want to maintain as much flexibility as possible. Just go ahead and set them when you have a hole in your schedule or when something necessitates you getting all your little minions in line. Besides, this keeps them on their toes in anticipation of their monthly one-to-one with you. Remember, unpredictability is key.

Unpredictability is where the brilliance comes in. They won't have any idea what you want to talk about, so you already have them on the defensive. Then tell them what you're upset about and see what solutions they have for you. If one of them has a good one, say that's exactly what you were thinking and then tell them that you really look at them as your second-in-command, regardless of whether you do or not. Saying this will puff them up and get them on your side, which is what you want. If they have something they need to talk about, tell them to schedule some other time with your assistant and make sure it never shows up on your calendar. Also be sure to tell them that you expect them to figure out their own issues because that's how you got to where you are, isn't it? Nobody helped you! Make them feel small for even asking.

Now, a critical point here is to make sure they know that what you discussed is a secret between you and them. Just to make sure they feel special, make a couple of snarky comments about some of the other managers so they know you really mean it. This is a great way to test who can be trusted and who cannot. If for whatever reason they start comparing notes, well, they have just violated your rules and they will not be in the inner circle for long.

The easy part of this whole process is that you simply rinse and repeat with all your direct reports. Since you aren't really planning on listening to anything they have to say, you can just sit back and work on improving your facial expressions and body language. Saying the same thing to each one is the point. They are never going to question what you say if they think they are the chosen heir. Just keep telling them they are! They are all the spokes to your hub, and your job is to make sure they never become a hub. That could be dangerous for you, and it's certainly not leader-like.

Wasn't that easy? Mentoring in thirty minutes or less, and you now have more time to hit the links! One final note on this: If you do catch your people comparing notes on the fact that you told several of them the same thing about them being your special manager or next in line for a promotion, or that you told them different things, deny, deny, deny. Ask them why they would spread rumors like that when, of course, you said no such thing. Question them as to how they could have possibly misunderstood! Then write them up. The key is to stop that spoke in its tracks. Put a stick in those spokes so the rider does a face-plant.

LET'S GET REAL

Having private meetings for disseminating public information creates a culture of mistrust. Meet with teams in groups of three or more. Never tell someone they are your *chosen one* or that they are in line for a promotion if they aren't. That's just mean and disingenuous. Mentorship is about the mentee, not you, so ask them how they want to grow into their leadership shoes and how you can help. This is not about *you*!

Being a leader is about being open and honest. Never letting others hear your conversations or sending different messages to Hub and Spokin' different people teaches a very dangerous form a leadership, one that is about mistrust and how to keep that value alive.

People do not behave their best in a culture of mistrust. In order to behave and perform their best, people need to know that the words of their leaders and fellow employees are honest and can be heard in the light of day. If something can't be aired in public and it's something the entire company should know, it should not be held in a didactic conversation.

Leaders grow with information, truth, and each other. Lead the way.

PREVIEW

"HOW (NOT) TO BUILD A GREAT TEAM"

How many times have you hired someone only to fire them a few months later? Worse, how many times have you not fired them and instead suffered silently in your regret and denial over a bad hire? Either way, a wrong hire can do lasting damage to your business, and more importantly, to the morale of the team upon which your business's success depends. Business strategies don't make great companies, people do.

Building a great team is hard work, and great interviewing and hiring is an art form that many leaders take for granted. In our next book, we'll take a look at some of the common and ridiculous mistakes, assumptions, and practices of leaders trying to build a well oiled team. And we'll shine an especially bright light on how to recognize when your latest hire is about to be shot by their own troops because you're not doing anything about it.

And again, we'll call leaders out on their propensity to make team building all about them and not about the team members. Many leaders are skilled sellers who want to be liked by people impress the interviewee with their brilliance. When they are done explaining how wonderful they are and how great the company is, they allow a little time to find out about the person in front of them. But they forget to ask the requisite questions that will help them predict future performance, and how the candidate will interact with and complement the existing team members. Not surprisingly, the savvy interviewee is astute at getting a hiring manager to look over here when they really should be looking directly at what they have already done that rises to the level of executive crimes and misdemeanors in bad management. Thus many leaders create a team of misfits that, instead of raising the level of performance in the organization, only succeeds in raising our blood pressure.

If you saw a little of yourself in *How (NOT) To Be A Leader*, we're sure that *How (NOT) To Build A Great Team* will help you put your better leadership skills into practice in a way that saves time, money, and the sanity of your most valuable team players.

ABOUT THE AUTHORS

Mary Marshall's passion is helping entrepreneurs and executives achieve their dreams. Mary has been a CEO, an owner, and chief cook and bottle washer. She's been a Vistage Chair (member and executive) and has coached leaders to find their own success. In 2014, she published her first book, *Putting Together the Entrepreneurial Puzzle: The Ten Pieces Every Business Needs to Succeed* as a collection of answers to the most common problems that hamper small business success. Marshall Advisors, LLC is Mary's consulting practice in Seattle, which focuses on strategic planning, CEO and executive coaching, and leadership development. Mary speaks on Intentional Culture for organizations nationally. Since 2012, she has been active teaching a course for the Small Business Administration called "Emerging Leaders" that takes entrepreneurs through a seven-month course to create a strategic growth plan for their businesses. The course is considered a mini MBA.

Kim Obbink is an Art Center College of Design graduate who began her career as a graphic designer and over the years became an accomplished brand strategist and leader. She worked as both employee and vendor for many worldclass technology and entertainment companies, and ultimately served as CEO of a Seattle based digital marketing and talent acquisition company. Her experience brings high-altitude vision and strong brand strategy to everything she does. Kim believes that an authentic brand requires authentic leadership. Her vision that values and a well-stated, well-actioned belief system are the religion of every healthy organization is what she brings to her consulting work with growth-oriented companies today. An entrepreneur, strategist, writer, and artist, Kim has a colorful view of the world. That combined with a bold sense of humor allow her to share her unique perspective on how others can find success and satisfaction in being great leaders from the heart.

www.ingramcontent.com/pod-product-compliance
Lightning Source LLC
Chambersburg PA
CBHW050326120526
44592CB00014B/2070